A BIBLE AND A PASSPORT

Dr. Jun Escosar is one of the leading voices in the world on evangelism and missions. Our friendship goes back to 1984 where he was among hundreds of students in Manila who met Christ as Lord and Savior. To signify they were taking the Great Commission literally, students purchased passports as well as Bibles. Since that time, Jun has never waned in his focus to reach every nation in our generation.

—Dr. Rice Broocks
Cofounder of Every Nation
Author, *God's Not Dead*

Pastor Jun has written a marvelous missions book! Here you will find the essential missiology of Every Nation as it has developed over the past twenty-five years. This book is a must-read for anyone interested in how missions movements begin, grow, and flourish!

—Dr. Larry W. Caldwell
Academic Dean and Professor of Missions, Sioux Falls Seminary, USA
Former Academic Dean and Professor of Missions
Asian Theological Seminary, Philippines

Jun Escosar's book on missions is a story of faith, hope, and love: the Great Commission. *A Bible and a Passport* is a timeless narrative of our involvement as Christians in reaching the next generation and discipling the nations.

—Senator Gringo Honasan
Philippines

We have been blessed by the writings of pastors from Victory and Every Nation, and here is another solid book, now coming from the pen of its very own missions strategist and resident missiologist, Dr. Jun Escosar. Stamped with Victory and Every Nation's brand of biblical, missional generosity, this is a Spirit-filled book on evangelism and missions, punctuated with heartwarming personal stories; one that will inspire and spur discipleship movements to thrive for succeeding generations.

—Dr. Tim Gener
Chancellor and Professor of Theology
Asian Theological Seminary, Philippines

If you are a Christian committed to the Great Commission, *A Bible and a Passport* is undoubtedly the most important book you will read this year. One part spiritual alarm clock and one part road map to mission, this book is an addictive page-turning seminar on what the Spirit is always doing in the world. I promise it will wake you from spiritual slumber and guide you on a journey towards the purposeful Christian life you long to live. Whether you are a new Christian or a veteran minister, you will not find a more inspirational missional guide than Dr. Jun Escosar.

—Dr. David B. Ward
Professor of Homiletics, Indiana Wesleyan University

This book is an essential textbook for anyone who seeks to have a dynamic and sustainable mission movement. It details the exponential growth of Every Nation Churches and Ministries as one of the most dynamic mission movements in the world today. It outlines the biblical principles on which this movement based its work and also provides a careful study of other great missionary-sending movements in church history. The most valuable lessons of this book derive from the stories and illustrations of Every Nation missionaries who have applied these principles in literally going into all the world over the past twenty-five years.

—Bishop Efraim M. Tendero
Secretary General/CEO, World Evangelical Alliance

This volume of Jun Escosar digs deeper into the mission, values, and characteristics of a young Christian movement. After reading through these pages, one finds that serving cross-culturally could be hazardous and yet fulfilling when the work is done in the wisdom, strength, and provision of the Holy Spirit. The leaders have concluded that the secret to their success is not the uniqueness of their strategy or methodology. Rather, the secret to their power is their compassion for the lost. Indeed, God can use any method out there, as long as love and commitment to the lost is modeled after Christ.

—Dr. Miguel Alvarez
Professor of Theology and Mission
Asian Seminary of Christian Ministries, Philippines

With many encouraging global ministry reports, Jun Escosar touches on three intersecting themes: discipleship, leadership, and multiplication. He aptly reminds us that we are called to make disciples that multiply, shape leaders that transform, and plant churches that plant churches. Jun unpacks the Every Nation story globally with wonderful testimonies of how God has moved in and through their movement. This wonderful story is underpinned historically and biblically to illustrate best practices that have led to a movemental Kingdom force to be reckoned with. Aslan is on the move, we have the Bible and a map, it's our move now!

—Dr. Ed Stetzer
Wheaton College Graduate School

I have known Jun Escosar for over twenty years; first as a pastor, then as a missionary trainer, and now as an author. *A Bible and a Passport* will challenge you to leave the ordinary life and get into the harvest. If you already have a Bible and a passport, then this is the blueprint you need on how to build a missionary training and sending program in any church, anywhere in the world.

—Gordon Robertson
CEO, The Christian Broadcasting Network

The nature and acts of God in Scripture can be summed up essentially in two ways: God is a missional and relational God. Dr. Jun Escosar captures these two facets of the Father's heart, the missional mandate to make disciples and a great compassion for the lost. The Lord's desire is that none should perish but for everyone to come to a saving knowledge of the truth. Pastor Jun imparts both the missional passion to proclaim the gospel in every nation as well as the love of Christ that compels us to be ministers of reconciliation.

—Bishop Manny Carlos
Chairman, Victory Philippines

A BIBLE AND A PASSPORT

Obeying the Call to Make Disciples in Every Nation

Dr. Jun Escosar

with Walter Walker

A Bible and a Passport
Obeying the Call to Make Disciples in Every Nation

Copyright © 2019 by Jun Escosar
All rights reserved.

For more information on sales, licensing, or permissions,
contact the publisher:

Every Nation Leadership Institute
P.O. Box 1787
Brentwood, TN 37024-1787 USA

Trade Paperback ISBN: 978-0-9752848-4-1

Printed in United States of America

CONTENTS

ACKNOWLEDGMENTS

There are a number of people I want to thank for getting this book into your hands.

First, I want to thank Pastor Steve Murrell who encouraged me to write this book. Our aim is to encourage our current and future Every Nation pastors and leaders to give Jesus' Great Commission an important place in our lives and ministries.

I want to thank Walter Walker, the man gifted by God to help me write this book and articulate in writing what we believe will be essential to motivate our members and leaders toward missional thinking and action.

Special thanks to Dr. William Murrell for his tedious work and invaluable feedback in helping to edit this book.

I want to thank and honor all our missionaries serving in the nations and campuses of the world. Your lives, testimonies, and obedience to God serve as an inspiration to us all. I dedicate this book to you and to all the unsung heroes of the faith who faithfully serve God in the most challenging harvest fields of the world.

I want to thank my entire missions team who embody the ideals of being better together: Michael Paderes, Jonathan Bocobo, Carlo Ratilla, Rodnel Gascon, and all our administrative staff that work diligently out of the overflow of their love for Jesus and the nations.

I also thank and honor Victory, starting with the leadership team: Bishops Manny Carlos, Ferdie Cabiling, and Juray Mora; Pastors Steve Murrell, Gilbert Foliente, Paolo Punzalan, and Ariel Marquez. I have had the privilege of serving with these men for many years. Their lives have inspired my walk with God. I am also grateful for the Victory pastors in Metro Manila and the Philippines that serve as mission ambassadors to their local churches and have tirelessly partnered with us in reaching the nations. Of course, we will not forget our generous church members and partners who support our missionary endeavors by sacrificially and graciously praying, giving, and going.

I also thank the Asia Leadership Team of Every Nation: Scott Douma, Timothy Loh, and Michael Paderes. Their friendship, insights, dedication, and sacrifice to serve Asia are over the top.

I also want to thank and honor the regional leadership team directors of Every Nation whose lives and service to God are exemplary. I get to interact and dream with these mighty men to see Christ glorified in the nations: Brett Fuller (North America), Phillip Steele (Latin America), Wolfi Eckleben (Europe), Sam Aiyedogbon (Central Africa), Roger Pearce (Southern Africa), and Rouel Asuncion (Middle East).

Thank you also to the faithfulness of Ms. Varsha Daswani and the Every Nation Philippines Communications and Technology Department who worked hard at editing, fact-checking, layout, designing, and printing of the book.

And of course, my family: my beautiful and faithful wife, Gigi, and my two wonderful children, Rachel and John Daniel. They are my joy and inspiration in life.

Above all, to my Lord and Savior Jesus Christ, whose very holy and perfect blood purchased men for God from every tongue, tribe, language, and nation, to You be all the glory!

FOREWORD

by Steve Murrell
President and Cofounder, Every Nation Churches and Ministries
Founding Pastor, Victory

Since I have known him, no individual has made more of an impact on missions in Every Nation than Jun Escosar. From the time I met him in 1984 in the early days of Victory in Manila until today, he truly honors God by his unrelenting passion to win the lost, make disciples, and train leaders. His heart beats to plant churches and campus ministries in every nation. Jun serves as the Asia Leadership Team director of Every Nation and an ever-present example to Every Nation missionaries all around the world. With that in mind, I talked to Jun several years ago about writing a book that would multiply his impact and leverage his influence worldwide.

I told him that he can't be everywhere at once. Quoting Habakkuk 2:2, I challenged him to inscribe the vision, that those who read it will be equipped and empowered to run with him. Though Jun reluctantly admitted that he couldn't be everywhere, no one has ever tried harder to do just that. In the last five years alone, he has been involved in fifteen church plants. Jun is a man of initiative and action who has always been more likely to be fully engaged in doing something rather than simply talking about it—or writing a book about it. As we talked about a potential book, I could read his thoughts as if he were shouting them from the housetop: *With so much to do, so many people groups and nations to reach, who has time to sit down to write a book?* However, the leadership team of Victory and I were equally determined. And so, to get Jun to focus on inscribing the vision to make disciples in every nation, we half-jokingly (but half-seriously) threatened to take away his passport. Well, that got his attention, and he finally agreed to write the book you now have in your hands. However, Jun's agreement came with one stipulation—that I would write a foreword briefly explaining the origin and context of the first five words of the Every Nation mission statement: "We exist to honor God . . ." That seemed like a good deal to me, and so I was happy to add my little story—at least the part I had to play in it.

CONTEXT OF THE MISSION STATEMENT

As a young campus missionary from Mississippi thirty-five years ago, I, along with my wife, Deborah, joined a team of sixty-five American summer missionaries on a mission trip to Manila, Philippines. We conducted evangelistic meetings during the first month of the outreach at the Girl Scouts Auditorium in Padre Faura, Manila. Jun had just graduated from college then and was living near the University Belt (U-Belt). It was July 1984, and we found ourselves having landed at ground zero of the revolution that would eventually end the twenty-year regime of President Ferdinand Marcos. Every day the streets around the U-Belt were filled with anti-Marcos protesters. I don't mean fifty people holding up signs in order to get on CNN; there were typically 10,000 to 40,000 people (mostly students) marching down C.M. Recto Avenue right through the heart of Manila's U-Belt, headed for the presidential palace. Consequently, barricades of coiled barbed wire and tanks with attached water cannons blocked the end of that street. A few of the new Filipino believers (including Jun Escosar) regularly shared their faith over a megaphone as students marched by with signs that read, "Down with the U.S.-Marcos Dictatorship." On a few occasions, soldiers fired shots into the crowd, and one student was killed not far from where we were set up.

Rice Broocks, my good friend and the leader of our summer missions team, preached every night for four weeks in the auditorium, which was packed to overflowing with around 600 students. My job each night was to take the fifteen to thirty new believers into a room on the side where I would explain the gospel again and pray for them to be baptized in the Holy Spirit. There would be a fleet of jeepneys available to take them straight to a hotel a few blocks away, where they would be baptized in water. The new believers would get back to their dorms about midnight.

Typically, after a final song, Rice would end the meeting and dismiss the students. However, on the tenth night of the evangelistic outreach, something quite supernatural happened. There was a second song, then a third and a fourth. After an hour the meeting was still going. I could hear shouts of praise and worship that just wouldn't stop—all happening while I was stuck in the follow-up room with the new believers.

When I got back to the meeting room, things were finally winding down. Those who understood where I had been immediately began saying to me, "Steve, you won't believe what happened! It was amazing! You should have been here!" Some of our more mystical team members described it as being a moment like that in 2 Chronicles 5, with the glory of God, smoke filling the room, and people unable to stand in His presence. Then hearing the same story from Rice, who leaned toward the practical as much as I did, I began to think to myself, *Why am I never in the room when supernatural things like that happen?*

ORIGIN OF THE MISSION STATEMENT

With one week to go before Rice and our team of American summer missionaries were scheduled to leave Manila, I was at 1880 C.M. Recto Avenue in Manila's U-Belt, sitting in my office—also known as Dunkin' Donuts. Deborah and I were staying an extra month to help train the new believers who would become the leaders of the fledgling church plant. Sitting at that Dunkin' Donuts, eating a munchkin, trying to inscribe our vision on a napkin, five words came to mind: **We exist to honor God.** I eventually added a few other things about evangelism, discipleship, leadership development, and stuff like that. However, those first five words were the easiest. The honoring of God is the ultimate issue in campus ministry, church planting, and everything else we were attempting to do.

I've often been asked about that five-word phrase and why I chose to say that "we exist to honor God," rather than the more traditional "to glorify God." The manifest glory of God is a very real thing but an experience that might happen once in a lifetime. I chose the phrase "to honor God" because glory seemed like such an easy thing to misunderstand. Experiencing God's glory can become very mystical. Honoring God as our ultimate intention seemed to make more feet-on-the-ground sense. At the beginning of the powerful movement we found ourselves in, I did not want us chasing the glory. I didn't want anybody to misunderstand that we exist for what happened in the Girl Scouts Auditorium on the tenth night. And so, in that moment, I chose the word "honor." We exist to honor God whether we're in a moment of glory or persevering in a dark and difficult moment; whether our efforts seem to be supernaturally empowered or we follow a disciplined approach that seems very natural; whether our experience is mundane or it causes the hairs on the backs of our necks to stand at attention. This is what I came up with at Dunkin'

Donuts that day: We exist to honor God by making disciples, training leaders, and planting churches in the Philippines, Asia, and the world.

The one-month stay in Manila for me and Deborah turned into twenty-five years as full-time residents. In 1994 (ten years after that moment at Dunkin' Donuts), Rice Broocks and our friend and fellow pastor Phil Bonasso stopped overnight at my house in Manila en route to Malaysia to scout out a church-planting opportunity. That night, we decided to establish what is now Every Nation Churches and Ministries, because it seemed that we could be better and do more together than we could apart. The questions that naturally followed were: What were we to do and why? The first five words still came as easily as in 1984 and now served as our starting point: We exist to honor God. The words that follow have been tweaked, edited, and expanded over the last twenty-five years, but the first five words have never changed:

We exist to honor God by establishing Christ-centered, Spirit-empowered, socially responsible churches and campus ministries in every nation.

PREFACE

I was fresh out of college in June 1984, moving from Iloilo City in central Philippines to look for a job in Metro Manila, which had a population of over six million at that time. That's when and where I put my faith in Jesus as my Savior and surrendered to Him as my Lord. The vision for world missions was planted in me in the first days of my life as a Christian. Pastor Steve Murrell and the other leaders told us early on that we needed two things as new believers: a Bible and a passport—a Bible to know God and a passport to obey Him. This served both as an inspiration and a challenge to us all.

From that time, young Filipino students who were becoming believers and disciples every day were inspired to envision themselves as missionaries. We were regularly challenged with the idea that all things were possible to those who believed—that one day God would use us Filipinos to make an impact in the world by taking the gospel of Jesus to every nation.

We started learning about what it meant to follow Christ by laying our hands on a tattered old National Geographic world map and interceding for the nations one by one. That became one of the earliest traditions at our church, Victory. Every time we gathered in our facility, that map on the wall would stir our hearts, reminding us that "God so loved the world, that he gave his only Son, that whoever believes in him should not perish but have eternal life" (John 3:16). The often-quoted Bible verse was Psalm 2:8 (NIV 1984): "Ask of me, and I will make the nations your inheritance, the ends of the earth your possession." Most of us were relatively poor young Filipinos who had never visited another country. Many had never been off the island of Luzon, where Metro Manila is. Few had ever seen a passport—much less possessed one. What an unlikely bunch to launch a worldwide church-planting movement!

But if we were to be that, it eventually occurred to me that we needed what Pastor Steve told us: a Bible and a passport. I couldn't go to the nations even if I heard the audible voice of the Lord asking, "Whom shall I send, and who will go for us?" (Isaiah 6:8). My response would have been, "I'm sorry, Lord, but I don't have a passport." So I gathered all the necessary documents, submitted the paperwork, and in 1986 obtained my first passport. That was an important lesson for me. If you sense God's calling, even as a passing thought, the best way to turn that impression into a clear sense of God's purpose for your life is to follow Christ by taking steps of faith in that direction. Obtaining that passport represented my first step of faith toward a life in missions.

Aside from the passport, I also needed to make sure I kept growing in my faith and relationship with God. From the early days of the outreach, we were taught the importance of reading and meditating on God's Word as a daily discipline. We used to say, "As long as you stay one chapter ahead of the other new believers, you can disciple them. If they get ahead, they can disciple you." Considering the comprehensive discipleship journey that we have developed at Victory over the years, simply staying "one chapter ahead" was, perhaps, an oversimplified approach to making disciples. However, for where we were at the beginning as brand-new followers of Jesus, that kind of simplicity was exactly what we needed.

When I finally received that first passport, I had no invitation, no apparent open door to missionary service, and no one offering to send me to the nations. But with a Bible and a passport in hand, I was ready to go. Over three decades later, I've had the privilege of ministering and preaching the gospel in over fifty different nations. And from the other young disciples who were challenged to envision themselves changing the world, Victory in the Philippines now has 185 long-term cross-cultural missionaries serving in forty-five nations. In the last five years, we've also had an average of 650 short-term missionaries serving in about twenty-three nations each year.

Over the years and along the way, the letters "DMiss" have been attached to my name, since I have completed a degree as a Doctor of Missiology. Occasionally, this has caused people to refer to me as "Dr. Escosar." However, I'm often unsure if they are serious. I don't approach life as an academic but as an advocate for Christ and the Great Commission. I never want to dig so deeply into sophisticated academics that I lose that first love—the simplicity of a passion for making disciples, praying over a tattered world map, and devoting myself daily to God's Word.

I now know that two things are needed to know and obey God—*A Bible and a Passport.*

INTRODUCTORY INTENTIONS

When I first signed up for this writing project, I envisioned it as a mere introduction to our vision as a movement to make disciples in every nation. Here's why.

My objective is to communicate that we are at the forefront of a very powerful movement. There are a lot of stories and strategy applications in the following pages. My purpose is to impart both the passion and procedures that have created the momentum we've been experiencing for several decades.

My perspective is that of a participant and observer, not a prophet. I can't tell for sure what the future holds or the context in which we will be sending out missionaries. It seems that much of the world is becoming an increasingly unfriendly place for Christians and Christian missionaries. I don't expect that trend to change culturally or politically, but I do expect people's hearts to become more and more open to the gospel. As I point out in Chapter 1, Jesus challenged those He sent out: "Look, I tell you, lift up your eyes, and see that the fields are white for harvest" (John 4:35).

My focus is not so much on the numerous theories of missiology as it is on the passion and practice of missions. The Great Commission, as expressed by Jesus in numerous passages of Scripture, is to go into all the world and make disciples of all nations. Practice is what makes one better at something. Over thirty years have gone by, and Victory in the Philippines is still practicing discipleship, still intent on getting better at it.

My expectation is that there will be other books on the Every Nation mission that will follow—books that will dig deeper into the mission, values, and defining characteristics of our movement. It's impossible to capture the Every Nation story in a couple of hundred pages. The movement is simply expanding too quickly. By the time this book gets published, there will have been at least six new Every Nation churches in Asia alone. I also don't consider myself to be one of those who can speak on behalf of Every Nation. In fact, though I have attempted to tell the amazing stories from Every Nation, much of my background and experiences are from Victory, our church in Manila, which is a founding member of Every Nation. My hope is that this will serve as a launching pad and an inspiration to our Every Nation churches around the world.

My highest concern is that we hold fast to the missional principles that will sustain this church-planting organization into the distant future. We are running a race that has been set before us, and we're all simply trying to keep pace with what the Holy Spirit is doing in our midst.

READER'S NOTE

Many of our missionaries are serving in what has come to be known as "restricted-access nations," which means that these nations are not only hard to enter, but if the objective is to preach the gospel and make disciples, it might be hard to stay for very long. We decided to use the term "creative-access nations" instead, because we believe that there's almost always a way to go into all the world and make disciples. It's rarely a matter of **if** we are to go, and always a matter of **how** we will get there. But it often takes a lot more than simply being creative—it requires divine guidance and supernaturally opened doors.

Some nations and people groups are extremely gospel-resistant. Consequently, publicizing the activities and impact of missionaries could create unnecessary security risks. In this book, names are often changed and places left unidentified. This is why no matter how detailed I will try to be, many of the greatest stories of the missionaries serving in Every Nation are the ones that will never be heard. They are our unsung heroes, and it is for their protection that their stories remain untold.

The purpose of the stories included in this book is not to promote individuals, but to demonstrate the power of the gospel and to illustrate how our unsung heroes are going into all the world in obedience to the Great Commission.

Spirit of the ...
... the Lord has anointed me
... good news to the afflicted,
sent me to bind up the brokenhearted,
... claim liberty to captives
... reedom to prisoners ...
... 61

1 THE CALL *to* EVERY NATION

We are debtors to every man to give him
the gospel in the same measure in
which we have received it.

— *P. F. Bresee*
  Founder, Church of the Nazarene

I am under obligation both to Greeks
and to barbarians, both to the wise
and to the foolish. So I am eager to
preach the gospel to you also who
are in Rome.

— *Romans 1:14,15*

01 Lord of the Harvest
02 Go and Make Disciples
03 Planting Church-Planting Churches
04 The Great Co-Mission

PART ONE

ESTABLISHED
1994

IN 1786, A YEAR BEFORE HE WAS ORDAINED AS MINISTER, William Carey made quite an impression at his first ministers' fraternal meeting of the Northampton ministers' association. The president of the association, Dr. John Ryland, asked the two new members to suggest a theme for the group's discussion. Perhaps the invitation was to impress upon the junior members how deep was the well of wisdom and knowledge among the established membership. The story is recounted for us from the testimony of Reverend Morris of Clipstone, who was present at the meeting:

> [Reverend John Collett Ryland, chairman of the association] invited the younger brethren to propose a subject for discussion. There was no reply, till at last the Moulton preacher (William Carey) suggested, doubtless with an ill-restrained excitement—Whether the command given to the Apostles, to teach all nations, was not obligatory on all succeeding ministers to the end of the world, seeing that the accompanying promise was of equal extent.[1]

Carey had been thinking about this for several years. At one point, he had been teaching geography and Bible lessons to schoolchildren to help support his family. It was the combination of those two subjects that gave birth to the missionary idea that set his soul on fire with passion and commitment to preach the gospel to those in foreign lands. Years later William Carey commented, "To know the will of God, we need an open Bible and an open map."

The aged chairman of the Northampton ministers' association sprang to his feet and thundered, "Young man, sit down, sit down. You are a miserable enthusiast for asking such a question. When God pleases to convert the heathen, He'll do it without consulting you or me. Certainly nothing can be done before another Pentecost, when an effusion of miraculous gifts, including the gift of tongues, will give effect to the commission of Christ as at first."

Carey sat down (at least outwardly) but the inner vision would not. In 1792, he published an eighty-six-page booklet entitled *An Enquiry into the Obligations of Christians to Use Means for the Conversion of the Heathens*, otherwise known simply as *The Enquiry*. In that same year, a group of five men, including Carey and the son of that same association chairman, Dr. John Ryland, formed what became known as the Baptist

Missionary Society. Each put in some money, pledged monthly support, and determined to solicit support from other interested parties. It was the first foreign missionary organization created by the British Evangelical Revival, known as the Great Awakening in the United States.

The Baptist Missionary Society organized regular prayer meetings and a penny-a-week contribution from each member for the support of foreign missions. As one biographer commented: "[Carey] came as near to the New Testament ideal of all Christians acting in an aggressive missionary church as was possible in an age when the Established Churches of England, Scotland, and Germany that had scouted (dismissed or ignored) foreign missions."[2]

The passion for missions comes from a compassion for those who have not heard that God so loved the world that He gave His only begotten Son, and that whoever believes in Him should not perish but have eternal life. It's not just an obligation for ministers, but a stewardship entrusted to **all believers** without ceasing, up until the great gathering at the end of the age. My hope is that every Christian and, for our part especially, every member of an Every Nation church would be faithful to that responsibility, whether they are called to pray, give, or go.

Think of it like this: through the substitutionary sacrifice of the Son, God has provided for us the most extraordinary gift—eternal life. By comparison, nothing this world has to offer has any meaning. But the gift was not for our benefit alone, it was for all mankind. God gave us a gift that was intended for the world. And therein lies the call and obligation—our stewardship. God gave us a gift that was meant for others as well, with the instruction to let them know. What a tragedy it would be if Christ gave Himself as a perfect sacrifice, and yet the ones for whom He died never had the opportunity to hear about it! Jesus Christ is worthy to have His story told to the last person in the last hut at the end of the last road. Our mission is to honor God by obeying Him and proclaiming His story in every nation.

Chapter 1

Lord of the Harvest

Expect great things from God. Attempt great things for God.

—William Carey
Missionary to India

"Look, I tell you, lift up your eyes, and see that the fields are white for harvest. . . . I sent you to reap that for which you did not labor."

—John 4:35,38

AFTER FIGHTING LONG, protracted wars with the French, the Americans, and the communist North Vietnamese army, the South Vietnamese army and government both collapsed, and Vietnam became the newest communist nation "on the bloc." That's an important distinction, because communist idealism tends to run its course and wear itself out after several decades. However, a communist administration, newly endowed with great power, can be among the most restrictive, brutally repressive persecutors of all—as bad as or worse than the dictators they overthrew. In Vietnam at that time, Christianity was considered something foreign and not to be welcomed. Its practice was banned, and Christians were persecuted.

My first trip to Vietnam was at the invitation of a few American missionaries who were attending one of our services in Victory Manila. They shared with me how the doors for ministry were closing for them in Vietnam. The systematic persecution of the underground church made it quite difficult and dangerous for foreign missionaries, particularly American missionaries, and any Vietnamese whom the secret police suspected of associating with them.

Since I am unmistakably Asian, the Americans asked if I would consider speaking at a series of meetings to Christians who desperately wanted to be trained for ministry. Every Nation had been wanting to plant a church in Vietnam, and what else could I say but "Okay, let's go!"? The trip would give me the opportunity to "scout out the land" and experience an underground Christian worship service in communist Vietnam. But, of course, there was no "us" in the "let's go"—just me.

I began to make arrangements for the trip, and three months later I landed in Ho Chi Minh City (formerly Saigon) in April 1996. As I checked into the hotel, I realized how far I was from Victory Manila, culturally and politically. I was asked (though I really had no choice) to register with the local police and surrender my passport. Handing over that passport really makes you aware of being at the mercy of a foreign power that is radically opposed to your very presence—even more so if they had known why I was in the country. Christian missionary work in 1996 Vietnam was much more intimidating than today because of the constant possibility of police raids. My contact person instructed me on the first day to assume a low profile and, by all means, to not speak English in public.

That same year, a fellow pastor and I made another trip to Vietnam. When we arrived at the meeting place, people were entering one or two at a time. A person behind the door watched through a small peephole to control the flow of believers arriving at and departing from the designated meeting place. That process seemed to work well—so well that I expected only a handful of Christians at the first meeting. When we were finally allowed by the monitors to come in, I was shocked to see over 200 believers packed like sardines in the living room. As we spoke through interpreters, the Vietnamese Christians received us with much warmth and openness. They were so eager to learn that they leaned in with intense concentration to hear and hang on to every word that came out of our mouths (actually, the translator's mouth). Speaking in a setting like that was quite an experience. Even the most fundamental teaching from God's Word seemed to set their hearts on fire. They were so hungry for the Word that we taught from the Scriptures non-stop for several days with only short breaks for lunch.

In the midst of their feasting on God's Word, the reality of the outside world was punctuated by a time of intense prayer. One of the lookouts spotted over a dozen policemen launching a highly coordinated raid just outside our meeting place. He stopped our meeting so we could intercede for those people. We were cautioned not to speak, but to just blend in with the locals if the police were to barge in. Perhaps it was our meeting for which they were searching. But by God's grace, after a moment of this silent intercession, the police went back to their cars and left. It's truly impossible to describe the intensity or the power of those prayers, even though our combined voices were no louder than a whisper.

Our contact picked me up the next day at the hotel and brought me to a group of Christians gathered in the business district of Ho Chi Minh City. We entered a store that sold a wide assortment of merchandise and proceeded to climb seven flights of stairs to the rooftop. Since the buildings were so close to each other, the Vietnamese believers (who were apparently used to such maneuvers) helped me make the short leap over to the next building. From there, we descended three flights of stairs in the adjacent building. All of this was a precaution. In the event of a raid by the police, we would not be in the building we had originally entered. We finally got into the designated meeting room where more than 100 believers were waiting to hear God's Word and be equipped as ministers. The hunger I saw for God's Word, the passionate worship, the intense intercession, and the courage to preach the gospel were unprecedented. It was like stepping back into the days of the first apostles as they proclaimed the resurrection of Christ in the Portico of Solomon and interceded with great fervor for the release of the imprisoned leaders.

Some preachers talk about persecution with a romanticized notion that it's good for the church and makes believers stronger. Though most of those preachers probably never experience real persecution, it just sounds good to say that the church grows despite the most brutal opposition. The reality is that the church often shrinks when it suffers. However, in the presence of great darkness—even demonically instigated darkness in which individuals and groups are enraged with uncontrollable hatred against God—the hunger for righteousness and truth grows stronger and stronger. Since that visit, I've had many opportunities to go back and minister in Vietnam. By the grace of God, as of 2019, Every Nation has thriving churches in five key cities of Vietnam which are planning to plant four more by 2024. What I learned from my first visit to Vietnam and hundreds of visits to missionary church plants around the world is that no matter how great the present darkness, if we only lift up our eyes, we will see fields that are ready for harvest.

THE HARVEST IS PLENTIFUL . . .

In the Samaritan village of Sychar, Jesus engaged a woman at the public well in a discussion. This account in John 4 comes in the early days of Jesus' public ministry, shortly after the wilderness testing and His separation from John the Baptist. This was apparently the first missionary venture into and among the despised Samaritans. The Jews hated Samaritans intensely and refused even to speak to them. The woman was shocked that a Jew would actually ask her for a drink. Jesus said that He had magic water (that is, "living water") and that if she would drink it, she'd never thirst again.

Word gets around in a small town like Sychar, and everyone knew this woman's story. Jesus knew it too, along with her deepest and darkest secrets. In the dialogue that followed, He revealed the truth about her life with her five previous husbands, as well as the sordid tale about her adulterous relationship with another man. Perhaps the dialogue went on for much longer than recorded in John's Gospel, because afterward she went out spreading the word about the man who had revealed "everything she had ever done." The result was that many of the townspeople believed because of the woman's testimony. Jesus spent two more days with the Samaritans and a great many more believed, saying, "We know that this is indeed the Savior of the world." Considering who those people were and how they responded, the impact of this first missionary contact with the Samaritans was remarkable.

Meanwhile, Jesus' disciples had gone out to get something to eat and, upon their return, were equally shocked that the Rabbi had been talking to the woman. In response to His bewildered disciples, Jesus used the quite unexpected events of that day as a teaching moment to challenge their thinking and expectations about the soon-coming harvest for the kingdom of God.

> "Do you not say, 'There are yet four months, then comes the harvest'? Look, I tell you, lift up your eyes, and see that the fields are white for harvest. Already the one who reaps is receiving wages and gathering fruit for eternal life, so that sower and reaper may rejoice together. For

here the saying holds true, 'One sows and another reaps.' I sent you to reap that for which you did not labor."

—John 4:35–38

In addition to their ethnic prejudices, perhaps the greatest difficulty the disciples had with embracing Jesus' vision for the harvest was that, from the beginning, they had seen themselves simply as helpers. A lot of their responsibilities related to crowd control (Matthew 19:13,14). Jesus was the Teacher, the Rabbi, and the great Miracle Worker. He was the one everyone was desperately trying to see. But what would happen to the crowds without the miracle-working Rabbi? Would they show up if it were just John, James, or Andrew—disciples and helpers, untethered from Jesus?

"Look, I tell you, lift up your eyes, and see that the fields are white for harvest." Jesus seemed to be challenging them to stop filtering things through the limitations of their own prejudices, inabilities, and expectations of where this movement might lead. He wanted His disciples to embrace a new missionary paradigm—one in which the harvest was seen as being white, abundant, and ready for reaping. That challenge was to prepare their faith to continue the ministry of Jesus as they went into all the world preaching the gospel.

Below are some ways we have applied the sayings of Jesus to the harvest that is white and ready for reaping.

The harvest is ready, even when the prevailing culture is not. Not long after sixty-five summer missionaries (mostly college students) arrived to plant a church in the U-Belt of Metro Manila, a veteran missionary spoke to the Americans about Filipino culture, including the rules and customs of automobile traffic. Traffic in Manila is unlike anything to which Americans are accustomed. Filipinos actually claim the right-of-way by simply not looking where they're going. To look is to surrender to oncoming traffic. It's jokingly said that in Metro Manila, green means "go," yellow means "go faster," and red means "go anyway."

The implied traffic rules of Metro Manila represent the implied rules of missions for preaching the gospel, making disciples, and planting churches. Many nations have the green light to do just that. Simply fill out some paperwork, and they'll give you a missionary visa. In other more restricted nations, the light has already turned yellow, and in a very short time it could turn red. These nations are quickly closing to the gospel. There's no time to hesitate. Jesus continues to challenge our missionary perspective, saying, "The fields are white for harvest; what are you waiting for?" We have to go faster in order to get there before they close. Many of the eighty nations where an Every Nation church exists would be categorized as "red" or closed nations (as of 2019). For security reasons, we blur faces of missionaries, delete specific references, or just don't report all that's happening. Consequently, many of the greatest stories of the Holy Spirit working through Every Nation missionaries may never be published. Red doesn't necessarily mean a nation is closed; only that missionaries gain access creatively. Missionaries called to these nations eventually find ways to go anyway.

Mike and Kim have been our missionaries to Vietnam since 1998. Mike knew that in order to effectively reach this highly restricted nation, the key was to raise local leaders who understood their culture and people. That strategy proved effective, and as leaders were equipped and empowered, the church began to grow in that city.

John was one of the young local Vietnamese pastors who felt it was time for him to step out in faith to plant a church in another city of Vietnam. Since there was a lot of tourism in this beautiful city, there would be zero tolerance for any type of religious activity. The local government was determined to rid the city of all churches. John had recently graduated with a law degree. Part of his motivation to be a lawyer was to know the local laws and be prepared to respond to any harassment from the authorities. The initial work began, and to their surprise, many young people responded to the gospel. Soon many gave their lives to Jesus. Even a fellow lawyer, John's former law school classmate, became a Christian and started actively attending one of the discipleship groups. He is now a campus missionary.

Ironically, all access indicators for planting the church in Vietnam displayed red. But John went anyway, even when the prevailing politics and culture were not ready. Despite many challenges and persecution, the church in that city has continued to grow. In fact, the momentum of the harvest was so great that they have planted a new church in a neighboring city.

We don't focus on numbers. The number of attendees is a third or fourth priority, particularly in more restricted or secularized regions of the world. An Every Nation church in Saudi Arabia with 100 members is equivalent to 10,000 in other parts of the world. What's more important is that the missionaries lift their faith to envision a plentiful harvest, white and ready for reaping—even in times and places where expectations are low. The church plants in Vietnam demonstrated that the harvest is ready, even if the prevailing culture is not.

The harvest is ready, even if the reapers are not. We are deliberate about helping people confirm their calling, assemble their teams, and develop their mission strategies. However, just when we think we've got the whole missions strategy and process worked out, the Holy Spirit will do something that shatters our preconceived notions of how churches should be planted. That's what happened with many examples from the early church, as well as with Joseph and Sarah.

Joseph and Sarah arrived in Qatar in the mid-2000s. Joseph worked as a purchasing officer in a semi-private company. Like all good disciples, they longed for fellowship and decided to start a small group, beginning with four other singles in their rented home. They had no idea that the six would soon grow to fifteen and then thirty. When they reached fifty attendees, with input from a missionary overseeing that region, they decided to have a weekly service in a small restaurant. Joseph really struggled, to the point of denying and questioning if this was really God's plan. He was quite unsure about his readiness to plant a church in Qatar.

The Holy Spirit continued to bring more people of other nationalities—Egyptians, Ghanaians, Indians, Kenyans, Lebanese, Nepalis, Nigerians, Sri Lankans, Thais, and many more. Joseph and the other leaders in Every Nation Qatar felt the need to move to a larger facility. The Lord provided a villa that could fit sixty to seventy people. When they already had two services and outgrew the villa, they moved to a function hall in a hotel good for 300 people. God continued to increase their number, and they moved to a secure worship facility within a religious complex that could accommodate even more. This is another example of how God's favor abounds, even in such a creative-access nation.

We have been astounded and truly humbled by the growth of the church in Qatar. As church planters and Christian leaders, neither Joseph nor Sarah felt ready or sufficiently mature. The harvest was ready, even if they were not.

The harvest is ready, even if you can't see it. Imagine a laborer sent out to reap, finding himself or herself standing on barren ground or among thorns and thistles, wondering: *What am I doing here? Nothing is growing because nothing was ever planted. I must have come to the wrong field.*

I wonder sometimes about Jesus and the disciples visiting the Samaritan village of Sychar. What if it had been the season in which nothing was growing? And what if, looking around, the disciples could only see barren ground? This might have been why Jesus said, "Do you not say, 'There are yet four months, then comes the harvest'?" (John 4:35). After all, why would He have said that if the fields were obviously ready for harvest? He continued, "Look, I tell you, lift up your eyes, and see that the fields are white for harvest." Whether or not that's actually what the disciples saw, Jesus challenged them to look at a barren field with eyes of faith and see the plentiful harvest.

My friend and I had the privilege of visiting Chittagong, Bangladesh, when the work was just starting in 1991. Because this was one of my earliest missionary trips to a Muslim nation, I made sure I was well prepared for the visit. I read a book of a well-known missionary to Bangladesh, devouring every page of his account as well as lessons he had learned from the field. However, my heart sank when I eventually learned that this missionary had served in Bangladesh for nearly thirty years and had seen only two converts. In my mind, if this veteran missionary could only realize a harvest of two Bengalis in three decades, what could we accomplish in our two-week visit?

Straight from the airport, we engaged six young Muslims that our local team had befriended. Five were students and the other was a son of an army colonel. We ate together, played badminton, and eventually preached the gospel to them. Quite to our amazement, each one of them had a dramatic conversion experience. Wherever I was invited to speak over those next two weeks, these young men were seated in the front row, hungry for everything shared from the Word of God. I had come to Bangladesh with the idea of two converts in thirty years planted in my mind. For us, that experience was just the beginning of a harvest in what is considered one of the toughest mission fields on the planet. In contrast to what I was originally expecting, it was an extraordinary harvest. However, it was not the result of better preaching, greater love, or a more engaging approach. Over time, there can be a kind of missionary rigor mortis that can set in. It begins as a hardening against great expectations, followed by a defense of unfruitfulness, jealousy of another's success, and eventually the criticism of those who are reaping a harvest. Going to a foreign mission field will challenge our faith in every way, and every missionary at some point will have the chance to stumble across those same pitfalls. Instead of guarding our hearts against high expectations, Jesus challenged His disciples (and we who follow in their footsteps) to guard their hearts against low expectations that will eventually lead to the other pitfalls. We need to see the field we're already in, or the one we're going to, as white and ready for harvest.

The harvest is ready for those who are sensitive to what the Holy Spirit is doing. Missionaries, particularly those laboring in what seems to be a barren field, need to develop the art of recognizing the Holy Spirit's work in a person's life. They should become like prophetic seers, listening intently to people's stories, looking for the signs of God's calling. Dr. Rice Broocks, cofounder of Every Nation and the evangelist who led the summer missions team in 1984, employs the SALT approach in his many conversations with agnostics, atheists, and non-Christians on campuses all around the world. SALT stands for: Start a conversation, Ask questions, Listen intently, and Tell the story. With the SALT approach, Pastor Rice has engaged the most ardent nonbelievers in meaningful dialogues about their personal beliefs. It is quite amazing how open people are to talking about the gospel when you learn how to talk **with** them, not **at** them.

Listening, learning, and looking for a sign is the approach that led a Bengali named Ali to Jesus. When our lead pastor in Bangladesh, Peter, first met Ali, he was wearing a long green turban and a long green robe, signifying that he was a Muslim religious scholar (*mawlana*). In their first encounters, it was clear that Ali was zealous and confident about his faith in Islam. In most of their conversations, Peter would not interrupt but listen quietly and patiently as Ali expounded on passages from the Qur'an. As this routine went on for over two months, Peter sensed that the finished work of Christ, the atonement blood of the sacrificial lamb, and the assurance of salvation were not only points of theological difference; they were clearly personal issues for Ali—evidence that the Holy Spirit was already at work in Ali's heart.

One day, Peter referred to a very sensitive topic from the Qur'an—passages that pointed to the deity of Jesus Christ (*Isa Al-Masih*) and the sinless life that He lived. In contrast, Peter also pointed out passages in the Qur'an on the life of Muhammad. After Ali carefully read those passages, Peter challenged him with the question, "How can someone save others when he has sins in his own life? Is Allah blind?" Ali left that day confused and disturbed by what he had discovered. After that day, he kept coming back, wanting to know more about Jesus from the Qur'an. In the process, their friendship was strengthened. Then one day, a couple of months after Peter had read passages that refer to the deity of Jesus, Ali came smiling and told Peter how he went through some religious books of Islam and found no evidence that could stop him from surrendering his life to Jesus, who is referred to in the Qur'an as sinless, a pure and holy one. He surrendered his life to Jesus and made the commitment to become His disciple. That was in August 2012. Today, Ali is serving full-time on the staff of Every Nation and is a key member of the regional leadership team.

Never is listening more important than when mission-minded Christians weave themselves into a foreign culture. Firstly, it invokes the principle of reciprocity. Listening closely, intently, and respectfully creates a sense of obligation among others to listen when we begin to speak. Secondly, listening gives us the chance to see the Holy Spirit's activity in their lives. Maybe we don't consider ourselves prophets or interpreters of signs, but it's not as hard as we might think. Maybe we're not looking at or listening carefully enough to people or to the Holy Spirit. That happens, sometimes, when we get too interested in what we want to say and not interested enough in other people's stories. Their stories often provide the key to opening their hearts and minds to the gospel.

The harvest is ready for those who act on the Holy Spirit's leading. In October 2018, the Every Nation churches in Oceania conducted the School of Empowerment in Brisbane, Australia. After one of the sessions, participants were encouraged to do some Spirit-empowered street evangelism. Two of our leaders from Every Nation Fiji decided to go to the campus. On their way, the Lord gave Ethan, one of our Fijian leaders, a vision of a man wearing athletic clothes, walking in a park near a fountain. The Lord also impressed upon Ethan that he was to tell that person, "Do not be afraid to use your talents." That was it—nothing so dramatic as a revelation about his secret affairs that would cause him to say (like the Samaritan woman at the well), "This man told me about everything I had ever done." Just a little encouraging word, "Don't be afraid to use your talents."

When Ethan and his accompanying team member Deral got to the Queensland University of Technology campus, they saw a man walking near the fountain, and they just knew that this was the guy in the vision. They followed him for about twenty minutes, but he was too fast, as he was quite tall. They never could catch up with him. It would have been much easier to give up the chase, but they pressed on and prayed for him to stop. As he continued to pull away from our Fijian leaders, the guy suddenly stopped as a large monitor lizard, common to the Brisbane area, crawled into his path. What should one do when God answers a prayer for intervention by sending a two-foot lizard into the path? In that case, Ethan was quick to say, "I saw you in a vision and felt like God had a message for you: 'Don't be afraid to use your talents.'"

The astounded man told them that he was a discouraged actor wondering if he would ever be contracted for a job in his profession. He was a Canadian tourist who had just arrived in Brisbane to attend a bachelor party. He said he had just quit his job but was afraid that he had made the wrong decision. He was also afraid that his talents would go to waste. At that point, they began talking about the love of God, the gospel, and God's purpose for his life. All three of them closed their eyes as they prayed together, and when they looked up they saw that the man was moved and encouraged to the point of many tears. They also saw that several students had gathered around them with their own prayer requests. It was a small gathering that made an extraordinary impression on everyone present—just the kind of intervention from the Holy Spirit that can lead to a plentiful harvest. They were in awe of the amazing God they served, as He had brought them away from their busy schedules in Fiji to Brisbane so they could pass on a message to a Canadian tourist.

The harvest is both already and not yet. Parables and figures of speech (John 10:6; 16:29) are metaphors that don't necessarily refer to actual events. The stories of the Prodigal Son and the Good Samaritan were probably just teaching illustrations to make a point. There may not have been an actual son who demanded his share of the inheritance or a Samaritan willing to help a traveler in need. On the other hand, there are parables that have prophetic significance, foretelling actual events that are destined to occur in both the near and distant future. Jesus' declaration that the harvest is plentiful is one of those prophetic sayings, referring both to what began with the outpouring of the Holy Spirit at Pentecost, as well as to what will surely occur at the end of the age.

From that point onward, Jesus would send and continue to send apostles into all the world to preach the gospel and make disciples of all nations. That was the already—the present application of the **Great Commission.** The not-yet fulfillment of the abundant harvest will be the **Great Ingathering** at the end of the age. The foretelling of that great gathering is recorded in numerous passages of Scripture. Below are just a few examples:

"And then they will see the Son of Man coming in clouds with great power and glory. And then he will send out the angels and gather his elect from the four winds, from the ends of the earth to the ends of heaven."

—Mark 13:26,27

"Then will appear in heaven the sign of the Son of Man, and then all the tribes of the earth will mourn, and they will see the Son of Man coming on the clouds of heaven with power and great glory. And he will send out his angels with a loud trumpet call, and they will gather his elect from the four winds, from one end of heaven to the other."

—Matthew 24:30,31

And another angel came out of the temple, calling with a loud voice to him who sat on the cloud, "Put in your sickle, and reap, for the hour to reap has come, for the harvest of the earth is fully ripe." So he who sat on the cloud swung his sickle across the earth, and the earth was reaped.

—Revelation 14:15,16

The blessing of Abraham to all nations, the Great Commission, and the Great Ingathering at the end of the age are all part of God's redemptive purpose in history. Each represents the promise of God that is both already and not yet.

GLOBAL MISSIONS CHALLENGE

The primary challenge to Every Nation leaders is to raise their expectations. How do you see the mission field: as sparse and barren, or as plentiful and ripe? In the early days of Victory Manila, Pastor Steve used to remind us regularly, "Don't be satisfied with small successes. As long as there is one person on your campus or in your city who has never experienced the grace of God in Jesus Christ, your mission is not complete." In other words, raise your expectations and keep them high. William Carey challenged the Reformed Baptist churches, "Expect great things from God. Attempt great things for God."

Pray for what's lacking. We can get really wound up praying for the nations and the great harvest of souls. But Jesus said that the harvest was already sovereignly prepared, plentiful, and ready for reaping. In another passage on the abundant harvest, Jesus said to His disciples, "The harvest is plentiful, but the laborers are few; therefore pray earnestly to the Lord of the harvest to send out laborers into his harvest" (Matthew 9:37,38). We need to be as earnest about our prayers for the Holy Spirit to send laborers as we are about our prayers for the harvest that is already plentiful.

Chapter 2

Go and Make Disciples

The purpose of an organization is to enable ordinary humans beings to do extraordinary things.

—Peter Drucker
Management Consultant

Him we proclaim, warning everyone and teaching everyone with all wisdom, that we may present everyone mature in Christ.

—Colossians 1:28

THE COMING OF THIS MILLENNIUM, also known as "Y2K," brought on a lot of technical and economic hysteria. The fear was that most of the computerized clocks that governed the modern world were incapable of counting beyond 99. At midnight on January 1, 2000, the modern world would technically revert to 00. Consequently, power grids would go down, financial institutions would lose records forever, and worldwide chaos would begin. People were storing food, building fortifications, and preparing for a cataclysmic system crash that would return us to the dark ages.

Christian leaders have also been known to put special significance on the turning of the calendar. Jules Michelet, a nineteenth-century French historian, painted a vivid picture of the year 1000 with prisoners, serfs, monks, and lords all awaiting the trumpet blast announcing the end of the world. However, Michelet's account was quite exaggerated, simply because in the middle ages there was far less agreement on what date or even what year it really was. There were indeed expectations of the final judgment in AD 999, but also in AD 899, 1199, 1299, and so on.[1]

In February 1999, a conference was held in Singapore billed as the "World Apostolic Summit." The attendees, who came by invitation only, were the leaders of great Christian movements from every corner of the globe. Pastor Rice had been invited but was unable to attend. Eventually, he prevailed upon Pastor Steve to go in his place. In the fifteen years I had known Pastor Steve, he had never once used the words "apostle" or "apostolic" with reference to himself. He's really not into titles.

None of the thirty representatives were expecting the return of Christ at midnight on January 1, 2000. However, they were asked to consider the question: What is God saying to the church at the beginning of the second millennium? Each leader in turn gave his prophetic insight on the question—many of the responses inspiring, some of them quite profound. Pastor Steve was the youngest in the circle and the only one wearing jeans. He commented later on how out-of-place he felt. When it was his turn to speak, he simply said: "I feel the Lord is saying to His church in 1999 the same thing He said in 1899, in 1599, in 999, and in 99: 'Go and make disciples.'" Apparently, he was the only one who said anything about discipleship. Pastor Steve recounted the story to us at Victory as a way of reinforcing the Lord's "standing order"—go and make disciples of all nations.

Almost every church group has some kind of statement about discipleship in their core values or organizational literature. "Discipleship," however, is often not very well-defined. Sometimes it refers to small fellowship groups or Bible studies within the larger church. For other congregations, it's a description of what happens in Sunday school or Christian education classes. In some churches it's understood to be the ministry of the Word in the weekly sermons. Still in others, discipleship is simply the statement of the overall ministry of the church, without any program specifics.

Many churches have been birthed with a strong commitment to discipleship, but as membership grows into the hundreds and thousands—or as the demographics change from youth to a community membership—the discipleship journey can break down. As a result, it can become increasingly difficult to incorporate mission-oriented discipleship. Since discipling thousands of people seems to be highly impractical, the commitment to making disciples becomes less and less defined—and less and less meaningful. And yet, this is precisely what Jesus has instructed the Church and its leaders to give themselves to doing.

Over the years, discipleship has been the central driving focus for Victory in the Philippines. As a result, we've gained some measure of success in that pursuit. Here's the short story of how we began with a strong commitment to discipleship, were overwhelmed with the wrong kind of growth, learned some valuable lessons, and emerged with a strategy that has empowered the members of our large congregation to effectively make disciples.

NEVER INTENDED TO BE ATTRACTIVE

From the initial missionary church plant in 1984, the team of American summer missionaries and their leaders were dedicated to winning unbelievers to Christ and making disciples. Pastor Rice preached in the nightly meetings. Team members presented the gospel throughout the day and invited students to join the meetings. Pastor Steve taught the biblical foundations classes. Everyone pitched in wherever they were needed. There was a great sense of urgency in those early days at the U-Belt in Metro Manila. Most of the American team members were college students coming from a strong discipleship culture. They knew their time was short, and their job was to train their replacements as quickly as possible. They were completely focused on training a group of very young believers to take over. "Leading with the idea of leaving," you might say, which is a good approach for making disciples.

It was never the team's intention to recruit Christians from other churches. That commitment was evidenced by Pastor Rice's welcome message to Christian youth groups visiting during the outreach: "Thank you very much for coming," he would say, "and we want to encourage you to continue to follow Christ. But please, don't come to these meetings. We're here to reach the lost, not to gather Christians."

As a brand-new Christian myself, I wondered why he would say such a thing. Even with his best efforts at being polite, asking them to stay away seemed a bit rude. Rude or not, banning other youth groups was simply because of the limited space in the Girl Scouts Auditorium where we were meeting and the team's commitment to winning those who did not know Christ as their Savior—not evangelizing the already-believing. With a revival in progress much greater than any of the missionaries had expected, Pastor Steve and Deborah, young pastors from Mississippi State University (with a full year's experience, even) stayed on in Manila for an additional two months—a commitment that eventually turned into thirty-five years and counting.

Within the first few years, Victory had grown to about 2,000 members. We were still as committed to winning the lost and making disciples as we had been at the beginning. However, we were growing at such a rate that the church was simply bursting at the seams. That was true of our two locations in Manila's U-Belt and the Makati Sports Club, but was also true of the wineskins that Jesus talked about in Matthew 9:17. He pointed out that old wineskins were not flexible enough to contain new wine that was fermenting and rapidly expanding. Eventually, the wineskins would burst and the wine would be wasted.

Church growth experts point to changing dynamics of churches as they grow through the 200, 500, and 800 membership levels. Of course, the challenges at those levels are missionally dependent—that is, the level of the challenge depends on the difficulty of the mission we are trying to accomplish. Drawing a crowd of 2,000 is one thing; making disciples of those 2,000 is a different thing altogether. The ministry that had sent those sixty-five missionaries was located on college campuses with congregations and student groups averaging less than fifty members. No one had any idea, let alone any experience, in creating a system of making disciples that would accommodate thousands of people. We were clearly out of our depth. Our challenge, and the turning point for Victory at this particular juncture, was whether we could keep making disciples—or become a church with a crowd of spectators, a large percentage of whom would follow at a distance and watch the rest of us preach the gospel and lead the church.

A CHURCH-PLANTING OPPORTUNITY

What seemed to be a great church-planting opportunity turned into a struggle that revealed some serious weaknesses in our ministry strategy. Pastor Steve received a call about a movie theater in a shopping mall that had been converted into a 1,000-seat performing arts auditorium. The owner was a new believer who wanted to rent the theater to someone who would start a church there. The man was told, "Call Steve Murrell. He'll start a church anywhere." Since we were out of space in our current location, using the theater sounded like an answer to prayer.

We asked 100 members of Victory Makati to help us plant a new congregation by attending and bringing their friends to a 4:00 p.m. service at the mall's theater, called the Star Complex. I don't know of another church in Manila that met in an upscale mall at that time. Consequently, lots of people began coming to see what was happening. Within a year, it was standing room only at the theater. Victory Manila now had three locations and about 3,000 people.

Our congregation at the Star Complex was very different from our first two. The church plant in Manila's U-Belt was founded with new believers from the student riots in 1984. The Makati congregation was likewise birthed through student evangelism. However, our Star Complex adventure was different. In contrast to the others, we had birthed that congregation by simply attracting Christians from other churches. At the time, two megachurches in Manila were experiencing leadership crises. Thousands had left those churches in search of a healthy church home, and many of them landed in Victory's new location at the Star Complex. That form of growth was never our intention. It's just what happens in some cities when a convenient location is combined with good music and preaching.

NEW AND IMPROVED WINESKINS

From the beginning, the commission to go and make disciples had been deeply imprinted on us by Pastors Rice and Steve, as well as other members of the American team such as Tom Bouvier and Al Manamtam. Though we seemed to be succeeding in ways that other churches celebrated or even envied, we knew something was very wrong. And we had no idea how to fix it. The more we grew, the more problems manifested themselves. As a result, the leadership team was forced to step back and take a long, hard look at what we were doing.

Prior to and during the whole Star Complex experience, our dear friend and fellow pastor Luther Mancao constantly pestered our leadership team with books and tapes on the cell church, a model that had become popular in the 1990s. Given the growing problems with Victory's latest church plant, we finally had ears to hear what Pastor Luther had been saying and were willing to give it a try. We engaged in a process that would lead to significant philosophical changes in the way we thought about planting and growing churches. There was no small amount of research, prayer, and discussion among Victory's leadership team. We commissioned one team to visit a church in Singapore that employed a small-group system of discipleship and learn everything about the thriving cell group ministry. Then we sent teams to South Korea to see what Reverend Yonggi Cho was doing. I was sent to the churches in Hong Kong and to the underground churches in China. Desperate to learn, we saw several things in our research and our travels that were worth incorporating—as well as a few things that became absolutely essential to our emerging discipleship strategy.

The process was important. All the members of our leadership team had to personally buy in to what we were attempting to do—that is, to create a discipleship culture and journey that would be effective and sustainable no matter how large Victory became. However, this was not a church-growth strategy. It was anything but that. We were committed to making disciples if that meant Victory remained small, or if we only discipled college students and consequently lacked resources. Pastor Steve expressed our commitment this way: "Small-group discipleship at Victory is Plan A; we have no Plan B."

Below are a few of the essentials that, over the years, have been deeply embedded in Victory's culture, philosophy, and discipleship strategy.

The One Essential Ingredient: A few years ago, people started flocking to Bogotá, Colombia, to learn about the G12 (groups of twelve) cell-group strategy employed by Cesar Castellanos and his 100,000-member international church, Misión Carismática Internacional. In 2002, we sent Pastor Ferdie Cabiling and Dennis Sy (who was not yet in full-time ministry) to study the Bogotá model for a few weeks. We had begun making plans to fly the entire leadership team of Victory to Bogotá when we discovered that Pastor Cesar was going to conduct a seminar in Singapore. Consequently, we all headed to Singapore and sat through every session. At the end of each session, we gathered to discuss what we had learned and how to apply it to Victory Manila. There were a lot of good principles, along with some that didn't feel right for us. And so we began the long process of incorporating one then another, tweaking this, adjusting that, and constantly evaluating the results. The most important thing we learned from Bogotá, as expressed by Pastor Ferdie in the summary report from his initial visit, was this: "The secret to their success is not their strategy or their process. In fact, we already have all the elements in place. It's just a matter of rearranging them. The secret to their power is their compassion for the lost." Rather than trying to copy their program, we tried to catch their spirit—their love and compassion for the lost.

Hundreds of pastors, church planters, and church growth consultants have visited Victory Manila over the years in an effort to download and install a similar system in their churches. And for several reasons, primarily this one, they have seen little success. Any effort to reproduce a comprehensive discipleship journey without a corresponding compassion and concern for the lost is destined to fail. Conversely, any congregation that is committed to preaching the gospel and winning the lost to Christ may eventually figure out how to develop an effective system. In Victory Manila, our objective in discipleship is not simply to turn good Christians into better Christians, but to turn nonbelievers into believers. Pastor Steve wrote about the competing philosophies of discipleship in *WikiChurch*.

> These two processes that headed in two different directions were simply the inevitable result of two different ideas about the definition and target of the discipleship process. For my friend and his leadership team, the discipleship process was designed to take care of the faithful, and their goal for small groups was to close the back door. For us, small groups are the front door to the church, and discipleship begins with nonbelievers.[2]

Small groups are often established in churches without the intention of engaging lost people for Christ. Not that they won't welcome new attendees, but evangelism is not their purpose. In the beginning at Victory, we didn't refer to small groups as care groups or life groups. We called them outreach groups because it defined our objectives better. Today we refer to them as Victory groups. There is still fellowship and discipleship that goes on in Victory groups, but small groups at Victory exist first to engage the lost.

Discipleship and Relationships: Many of the evangelistic conversions recorded in the Acts of the Apostles resulted in the conversions of entire families and households—Cornelius and his household (Acts 10), Lydia and her household (Acts 16), the Philippian jailer and his household (Acts 16), and Crispus and his household (Acts 18). Evangelism works best through relationships.

As we began researching on discipleship programs in the wake of our Star Complex church-planting adventure, I was sent to learn from a network of underground churches in China. I visited an old friend who was working with another mission organization in southern China. The ministry he was part of was doing small group meetings in homes. The small group I visited was composed of men and women between the ages of eighteen and thirty-five. Of course, language was a barrier. Even when they tried to describe how they did discipleship, the terms and concepts were hard to translate. I kept looking for the program—trying to get a handle on their discipleship strategy. I finally realized that there was no program, at least not one that I could point to and say, "This is how they make disciples." In fact, the way they conducted their small groups seemed odd and at times even superficial. They would begin with an icebreaker—some corny question to discuss. As it was being translated, I thought to myself, *I came all the way to China for this?* And yet they produced disciples whose compassion for the lost, courage to preach the gospel, and willingness to suffer for His sake were unparalleled. I discovered that small groups or house churches for the Chinese were much more about lifestyle, community, and shared life than intellectual discussions or Bible study programs. That's what seemed to be infusing life into their small groups. What I felt during that first visit to China was that we needed a transferrable system so that every Christian felt equipped, confident, and responsible to engage lost people, especially in their circles of influence.

In the years since that first visit, I've been back to China more than a dozen times. Each time, I am impressed by their passion for God and their relationships with one another. Just like in the book of Acts, the gospel works best through relationships. There are, indeed, Christians who have a special gift for reaching out to total strangers. However, the majority of Christians are called to reach lost people in their circles, who, in turn, can be equipped to effectively reach out to their own circles.

This is a typical story, one we have seen hundreds of times over in our Philippine churches. One member of the family gets saved, and soon brothers, sisters, parents, and cousins start coming to Christ and to the church. This is the context of evangelism for our Asian churches and in the unregistered churches in China.

Small-Group Discipleship in the Context of Evangelism: It's actually difficult to pick a starting point to describe the Victory discipleship journey because small-group evangelism and discipleship is a revolving rather than a linear process. In other words, it's a never-ending cycle that is constantly turning over and repeating itself. Those who are equipped to minister are very quickly empowered to begin engaging the next wave of unbelievers by inviting them to their Victory groups.

Since I have to begin somewhere in the discipleship journey, I'll start with church members **engaging** nonbelievers to start a conversation about the gospel, and probably asking them to attend a Victory group. We use a booklet called *ONE 2 ONE* that helps them go through the foundations of the gospel and the Christian faith. It covers seven basic but vital topics—salvation, Lordship, repentance, baptism, devotion, the church, and discipleship. There is also an app with several translations.

If these new believers make the decision to receive Christ as their Lord and Savior, they are eventually invited to participate in a *Victory Weekend*. This is the beginning of what we refer to as **establishing** believers in the faith, the Word and prayer, and church community. The sessions in these one-and-a-half-day events repeat some of the foundational teachings. There are also times of encouragement, vision-casting, and personal ministry. In one of the final sessions, new believers are encouraged to make a list of unsaved friends to invite to an upcoming small group. Those names become a matter of committed prayer over the following weeks. Aside from *Victory Weekend* to establish believers in the faith, the other tools in this phase of the journey are *The Purple Book* class (to be established in the Word) and the *Church Community* class (to be established in the church).

The next two phases of the journey involve **equipping** believers to minister and **empowering** them to lead by stepping out in faith to engage their friends with the gospel. This is usually done through *ONE 2 ONE* or in their own small group. Those who are busy, or not yet ready to lead a Victory group, can team up with an active group leader. Seeing unbelieving friends engaged with the gospel emboldens interns in a Victory group and propels them to lead their own groups. The tools in this phase are *Making Disciples* and *Empowering Leaders*.

The third and fourth phases are interrelated—that is, one cannot be accomplished without the other. Maybe new believers will be empowered to lead small groups without being equipped or given tools to be successful. Or consider the more common scenario—a new Christian sitting though years of sermons, seminars, and trainings without being empowered to engage unbelievers through a small group. Equipping and empowering are both necessary.

There are several more levels to equipping in the Victory discipleship journey to enable believers to start their own Victory groups. Small group leaders can attend a leadership group of four or five other leaders once a month, led by a more experienced Victory group leader. They can also enroll in *Leadership 113*, a ten-month leadership-training course designed to prepare and equip Victory group leaders to be more effective in ministry. It gets its name from 2 Timothy 1:13—"Follow the pattern of the sound words that you have heard from me, in the faith and love that are in Christ Jesus."

There's a deeply embedded philosophy revealed in this journey, particularly when joining discipleship groups, leadership trainings, and mission trips. As previously stated, a burden for the lost is a prerequisite for an effective pattern of discipleship. Likewise, one of the fundamental philosophies of discipleship for Victory is that a missional lifestyle (regularly engaging nonbelievers with the gospel) is necessary for spiritual growth and maturity in Christ. This is an uncommon approach, but we are as committed to that strategy as we are to making disciples. It's how we go about fulfilling the Great Commission. That commitment is reflected in the discipleship journey that has developed over the past few decades.

Sustainable Patterns of Discipleship: Those who had become Christians in the first few years of our church had all bought in to the idea of equipping the next leaders through small group discipleship. This is what we were born into as new Christians. However, as the church grew, we represented only about a third of the congregation. The question we were facing was: How were we going to impart that vision to the rest? More importantly, how could we equip regular church members to have compassion for the lost, preach the gospel effectively, and make disciples? We knew that those who lacked that compassion had only to experience leading someone to Christ to change that. What we needed was a journey that would enable each of our members to effectively engage unbelievers with the gospel, establish them in the faith, equip them to minister to others, and empower them to make disciples.

Church leaders often make the mistake of reading a book or going to a seminar, picking up new ideas, and then announcing these changes to the entire church. Typically, we are in search of a magic formula for church growth, financial stability, or greater membership commitment. If the changes don't work as well as advertised, we adopt another strategy or simply revert to the old way of doing things. It only takes two or three such sidetracks for followers to lose confidence. It's like making deposits and withdrawals from your leadership account. Every significant change in your ministry strategy is like a withdrawal on that account. Repeated withdrawals without significant deposits can result in a negative bank balance in relationships.

As Victory began to gradually shift its emphasis from large events to small group discipleship, the leadership team felt that we were about to stumble across something big. However, nothing was said from the pulpit about the changes we were making for almost two years. All the pastors and staff simply started making disciples in small groups rather than one on one. When someone would hear about a small group and ask if they could join, we would tell them, "No, you can't join one, but if you will gather three church friends and three un-churched friends, we will teach you how to lead one. When would you like to start?"

A FINER POINT

As much as Every Nation values discipleship, we all have different strategies for it. In the Philippines, Victory expresses it through the 4Es:

> **Engage** culture and community
> **Establish** biblical foundations
> **Equip** believers to minister
> **Empower** disciples to make disciples

Effective disciple making must include these four components. I believe that these principles will work in any context, but also recognize that they are applied differently from culture to culture and from nation to nation.

For decades, Victory's leadership team has been carefully measuring and monitoring our effectiveness in each of those Es. We understand that no process or system is static, and if left alone it will tend to erode—"entropy," they call it. Consequently, every system and process needs to be monitored and periodically tuned up. We've also discovered over the years that how and what you measure are almost as important as what you intend to do. While we count the number of people attending our services, that is the least important. Since our prime objective is to win people to Christ and make disciples, the numbers that really matter are baptisms and small group leaders. Whenever we had allowed our attention to divert to other numbers, our ministry effectiveness began to decline. It is true what they say, "What you measure and monitor improves." Let me put a finer point on those strategic commitments.

Engaging culture and community means we engage people with the gospel, the goal being to lead them to saving faith in the sacrifice of Jesus Christ. We affirm that discipleship is founded on relationships, and there are certainly times when we are compelled to persevere with people, even when they are reluctant. However, those with a ministry strategy of friendship, or relational evangelism, are often satisfied with simply befriending unbelievers. No matter where in the world we are operating, our objective is to continually and progressively nudge people toward an experience and an ongoing relationship with Jesus Christ. The first step in that direction is for them to hear the gospel and put the full weight of their trust in the atoning sacrifice of Christ.

Establishing biblical foundations means we understand that Christian doctrine matters. The primary questions we address are who Jesus Christ is and what He has done for us. That might be considered a radical reduction of Christian theology, but those doctrinal essentials provide a good foundation upon which to build. In regions of the world where non-Christian religions dominate, establishing biblical foundations can take more time and cover different topics. This is true whether the new believer comes from a secular-humanist background in Canada, a Hindu background in Nepal, or a Buddhist background in Myanmar.

Equipping believers to minister means we give them enough training for them to take the next step of faith. Our job as pastors is not to do all the work of the ministry. Rather, it is to equip every member to minister. Along with basic Bible study, we equip believers with practical ministry training and an abundance of learning experiences. Believers gain maturity by doing the work of the ministry, not just reading books and attending seminars. They tend to grow as they go. The myth of maturity, on the other hand, is the belief that new believers must have attained a high level of Christian experience and maturity before they are qualified to minister. Sadly, it's not uncommon for young people in other ministries to receive Christ as Lord and Savior, sense a call to ministry, and spend the next decade in preparation for leadership. Though we encourage advanced theological studies, some may never make it through such a long equipping phase. At Victory, we encourage new believers to engage in the work of the ministry early on.

Empowering disciples to make disciples means we create the tools, training, and programs that enable believers to successfully obey the Great Commission. It also means that we don't hold new believers back, but intentionally empower those we think have the potential to succeed. Their faith and confidence are always being stretched. We're not afraid of young believers making mistakes. We embrace this as an essential part of the discipleship journey.

FROM PRINCIPLES TO PRACTICE

Every cultural setting is unique and requires a corresponding approach to making disciples. The particular strategy used at Victory in the Philippines may not be as effective when used in other regions of the world. We've tweaked the journey along the way, but our strategic objectives for making disciples have remained unchanged: Each Every Nation church and campus ministry needs to develop its own ongoing way of engaging unbelievers in the culture and community, establishing biblical foundations, equipping believers to minister, and empowering them to make disciples. Here are a few examples of how Every Nation churches around the world have developed their own responses to existing cultural and political realities while making disciples.

Churches in Europe, Latin America, North America, and South Africa often use *THEGODTEST* as a means of engaging people on campus and in the community in a dialogue about God and the gospel. That is typically followed by a study of *The Purple Book* as a first step in establishing biblical foundations, and then by something similar to a *Victory Weekend*.

In eastern nations where the dominant culture, worldview, and religion are non-Christian, engaging people in meaningful dialogues that lead to God and the gospel takes a different approach. For example, our church in Nepal uses prayer gatherings as opportunities to introduce the power of God and demonstrate His supremacy over the spiritual world.

Several churches, such as those in Bangladesh and Guam, intentionally engage nonbelievers by sharing meaningful conversations about God and the gospel over meals and during social gatherings. In fact, many have encountered Christ at those dining tables.

Establishing biblical foundations also has a different starting point and deals with a different set of issues. Our churches in China have introduced even more basic lessons in their foundations classes for new Christians, beginning with a series on the topic "Who is God?" Our church in Malaysia has a similar approach, introducing a series of lessons on "Discovering God." And, of course, equipping new believers to effectively communicate the gospel within a Muslim-majority culture is quite different from equipping disciples to engage secular humanists and agnostics in New York.

Contextualizing the 1st E in Singapore

At the beginning of 2018, Every Nation Singapore began to work on a contextualized approach to engaging their culture and community. They regularly reached people from a wide variety of religious world-views—Buddhists, Taoists, agnostics, atheists, and freethinkers. They eventually discussed concepts like the sinful nature, the only begotten Son, and the authority of Scripture; but those are not ideal places to start a conversation. They saw the need to engage in a relational context—an approach that was perceived as adding value to the Singaporean people. They discovered that one possible starting point for evangelism is the idea of values. Most have heard of IQ (intelligence quotient) and maybe EQ (emotional quotient). In Every Nation Singapore, church members invite unsaved friends to a discussion about SQ (spiritual quotient)—the abilities and values that enable individuals and families to experience abundance. If a friend is interested in learning more, they are invited to a small group called *SQ-Values*. The first three sessions are discussions on the importance of values and the diminishing sense of value in things already obtained. All of this leads up to a full explanation of the gospel and abundant life in Jesus. From there, the small group continues in the process of establishing biblical foundations, equipping believers, and empowering them to engage their friends with the gospel.

4Es AS ORGANIZATIONAL CULTURE

In the Philippines, we've been making disciples using the 4Es since the early 2000s. We've tinkered and tweaked things along the way, but we never deviated from our overall strategic objectives. The questions and considerations are always the same: How can we more effectively engage unbelievers in their culture and community, establish biblical foundations, equip believers to minister, and empower them to make disciples? Is "the Victory approach" to making disciples now perfected? Hardly, and it would be silly to think so. If the leadership team briefly takes their eyes off the objective, they'll begin veering off into one ditch or the other. Monitoring our effectiveness and diligently seeking God's wisdom at every move are never-ending efforts.

That said, a great deal of momentum has been gained over the years. We're no longer struggling to create a system by trial and error. As a result, we've been able to develop and consistently reinforce a clearly defined culture of discipleship. The 4Es are all that most of us in Victory have ever known, so we continue in the journey of following Jesus and helping others follow Him with great ease. As a church, we just assume that's what new Christians are supposed to do. Whenever I think through this discipleship journey, I'm reminded of a quote from the famous management consultant, Peter Drucker: "The purpose of an organization is to enable ordinary human beings to do extraordinary things."[3]

GLOBAL MISSIONS CHALLENGE

The final instructions from our Lord were: "Go therefore and make disciples of all nations, baptizing them in the name of the Father and of the Son and of the Holy Spirit, teaching them to observe all that I have commanded you. And behold, I am with you always, to the end of the age" (Matthew 28:19,20). Among the greatest and most important challenges for all missionaries, cross-cultural or local, is making disciples in a way that is easily transferable, culturally relevant, and relationship-oriented, which will remain effective no matter the size or diversity of the church.

That doesn't happen overnight. We understand that what works in Manila or Cape Town might be inappropriate for Dubai or London. Even missionaries that were trained in Victory Manila have to tweak and fine-tune the journey to make it work in other cultures. Each cross-cultural and campus missionary should contextualize the 4Es, taking into consideration the culture of their campus, city, or nation. This requires "cracking the missional code" in order to effectively engage unbelievers in their culture and community, establish biblical foundations, equip believers to minister, and empower disciples to make disciples.

Chapter 3

Planting
Church-Planting Churches

You then, my child, be strengthened by the grace that is in Christ Jesus, and what you have heard from me in the presence of many witnesses entrust to faithful men, who will be able to teach others also.

—2 Timothy 2:1,2

"With what can we compare the kingdom of God, or what parable shall we use for it? It is like a grain of mustard seed, which, when sown on the ground, is the smallest of all the seeds on earth, yet when it is sown it grows up and becomes larger than all the garden plants and puts out large branches, so that the birds of the air can make nests in its shade."

—Mark 4:30–32

MISSIONS FOR EVERY NATION can be thought of as three ongoing initiatives: making disciples who are equipped to make other disciples, training leaders who can train other leaders, and planting churches that will plant other churches throughout their respective cities, nations, and regions. That's how the gospel advances. Throughout the centuries, that's how it has always advanced.

Turning those initiatives around, we also say that if we don't engage the lost, we can't make disciples. If we don't make disciples, we can't train leaders (discipleship and leadership training are not the same). If we don't have trained leaders, we can't plant churches that make disciples, train other leaders, or plant other churches. And if we do not intentionally and consistently grow by planting new churches, we can't sustain a healthy movement. The health of a church-planting organization is demonstrated not by weekly attendance, but an intentional approach to disciple making, leadership training, and church planting.

Stated that way, our vision can sound rather mechanical. In practice, both strategic and organic approaches are necessary, especially as our churches mature. In order to be intentional and focused in our church plant initiatives, we've plotted out the nations in Asia we want to reach every year. However, we would have no workers to send unless we have a functioning leadership pipeline. We make disciples and train leaders in a systematic way, but we go into all the world to plant churches only when individuals and couples have a clear sense of God's calling. In other words, we can't just plan our strategy for going to every nation. We plan around when and where the Holy Spirit leads church planters and missionaries to go. Sometimes we even need to plan around their experience, spiritual maturity, and readiness to go. That must be the reason the Lord instructed us to "pray earnestly to the Lord of the harvest to send out laborers into his harvest" (Luke 10:2).

If we think of church-planting organizations in terms of a biological model, the life and health of an organism (or an organization) are measured by its ability to grow and reproduce. To say that churches and church-planting movements are either dying or reproducing would be an oversimplification. Perhaps the idea is better expressed this way: churches are either newly born, healthy, or struggling to get strong or well enough to survive and reproduce.

THE ANTIOCH MODEL

The church in Antioch was established around AD 35 as Greek believers scattered throughout the Roman Empire, fleeing the persecution that arose after the stoning of Stephen (Acts 11:19). Antioch, the capital of Syria (modern-day Turkey), was a strategic city with a population of half a million residents, located at a major crossroads of commerce and education. By the mid-thirties of the first century when Jesus-believers arrived, it was the third most important city in the Empire, only behind Rome and Alexandria. It was there that believers were first called "Christians." It was also in Antioch that the Holy Spirit instructed the elders to set Paul and Barnabas apart, lay hands on them, and send them out to transplant the gospel. In the years that followed, Antioch became the primary church-planting center that established Christianity throughout Asia Minor.

Our mission and strategy seek to mirror what happened in Antioch in several ways.

Origins: There was no strategic plan to plant a church in Antioch. It was simply established as believers fled for their lives from persecution. In the same way, our church-planting initiatives are directed by the Holy Spirit as He moves in the lives of Every Nation church members. We don't send people by commanding them to go. We can only move forward as they answer Christ's calling, "Here I am, Lord; send me." Yet looking back, after two and a half decades, I'm amazed to see how far and wide that process (preparing and waiting on the Lord's calling) has taken Every Nation. We now have churches in eighty nations in twenty-five years, and this is not because we are good at planting churches in many parts of the world. I truly believe that the Holy Spirit has designed us to go into all the world to make disciples of all nations.

Missionary-Sending Vision: Ironically, Saul of Tarsus (from whom the believers had fled) became a believer, and thirteen years later was brought to Antioch by Barnabas. From there, the elders sent Saul (a.k.a. Paul) and others on several cross-cultural missions initiatives throughout Asia Minor and Europe. The Antioch church was one of the premier missionary-sending churches of the early Christian movement. Don't overlook its significance. That congregation was birthed by those who had fled for safety. They could have settled for a local vision, satisfied to fulfill it within the relative peace and prosperity of metro-Antioch. However, they were one of the first to embrace the vision of systematically propagating the gospel to the ends of the earth.

Regional Church-Planting Centers: No one knows how many other teams were sent out from the church in Antioch. What we do know is that while the Apostle Paul journeyed westward, others went to the east, birthing church-planting movements in modern-day Iran, Iraq, and Persia. We also know that Antioch emerged as one of the five regional centers of Christianity by the end of the first century, along with Jerusalem, Ephesus, Alexandria, and Rome.

Today, there are numerous church-planting movements all over the world. We certainly don't consider our progress in Every Nation comparable to or at par with what happened in Antioch. The church in Antioch, along with its members, has an irreplaceable position in the history of Christianity. That being said, we plant churches both strategically and organically as the Holy Spirit leads people to go (or flee); we continually send church planters all over the world; and we have seen a growing number of regional church-planting centers emerge within Every Nation.

EVERY NATION CHURCH-PLANTING CENTERS

We are committed to the vision of planting churches that have the same spiritual DNA as the congregation in Antioch—churches that are born with a passion to plant other churches throughout their respective regions and the world. Since Every Nation exists to honor God by establishing Christ-centered, Spirit-empowered, socially responsible churches and campus ministries in every nation, here are a few examples of how our mission has moved forward in the past decades, particularly through some of the regional church-planting centers that have emerged. However, this is far from being a complete list, and there are no limitations to it. Our vision is that all Every Nation churches will become church-planting centers.

Victory—Manila, Philippines
Established 1984

An early version of Victory's mission statement read: We exist to honor God and advance His kingdom by making disciples, training leaders, and planting churches in the Philippines, Asia, and the world.

We understood from the very beginning that the only way to effectively reach a nation was through planting church-planting churches. I'm not sure how we came to that conclusion. It seems to have simply been part of the spiritual DNA imparted to us by Pastors Rice and Steve. We were never tempted to establish a megachurch; we wanted to meet in several locations to make church accessible to our members spread out all over the city. Victory Manila currently meets in forty-nine locations. Outside Metro Manila, Victory has planted 100 churches all over the Philippines. This would not have happened without a crystal clear vision and mission. Otherwise, we would probably have fallen into the trap of simply building gigantic structures and trying to maintain local megachurches.

In the early days of Victory, new believers were encouraged to embrace the vision for world missions by reading the Bible and getting a passport. At that time, nothing could have seemed further beyond our reach, since most of us were relatively poor and few had ever traveled. Nonetheless, in 1986, we took another step forward and began sending short-term missionaries and long-term church-planting teams to the nations. As of this writing, we now have Every Nation churches in fifty-three of the sixty nations in Asia.

Third-generation churches are those churches that have been planted by churches that were planted by another church. If you think of church planting in terms of children and grandchildren, Victory Manila would then have twenty-nine children, fifty-six grandchildren, thirteen great-grandchildren, and two great-great-grandchildren—in all, 100 churches will have been planted throughout the Philippines by this year. Aside from these, Victory has also planted churches in nations such as Armenia, Bangladesh, Cambodia, Myanmar, Nepal, and Pakistan.

King's Park International Church—Chapel Hill, North Carolina Established 1985

In the autumn of 1984, Tom Jackson was a freshman at the University of North Carolina in Chapel Hill, North Carolina. He was walking across campus with Ron Lewis, who was leading a campus ministry that began with a three-week series of evangelistic meetings led by Pastor Rice. Drawn to the faith and vision of the campus ministry, Tom had joined this small group of students and recent graduates that met on the campus. He still recalls what Ron Lewis said as they passed between Hanes and Carroll Hall: "Tom, do you know why I like working with students? It's because when I say that we're going to plant churches all over the world, you guys believe me."

That's exactly what happened, and in ways neither of them could have imagined. In 1990, the church moved off campus (relaunched and eventually renamed King's Park International Church) and became a community-based church for students years before Every Nation existed. Today, King's Park is centrally located in the greater Raleigh-Durham-Chapel Hill area. Campus missionaries from the church continued engaging students with the gospel, making disciples, and training leaders in area campuses, including the University of North Carolina, North Carolina

State University, Duke University, North Carolina Central University, and Meredith College.

Soon the dream to plant churches became a strategy to plant churches. Several church-planting initiatives were birthed out of King's Park, each headed by disciples and leaders who were initially reached on one of the campuses.

In Europe, Tom and Jean Jackson, Jeff and Ana Bullock, and Mike and Myra Watkins planted churches in Ukraine, Scotland, and Poland. Taylor and Elizabeth Stewart planted a church in Guam, which continues reaching the islands of Micronesia. University of North Carolina graduate students KC and Hope worked with Ron Lewis and started churches in China and Taiwan. Simon Suh, a graduate of North Carolina State University, eventually became an associate pastor at King's Park for several years and established the Every Nation church in Seoul, South Korea. Some of those he reached established "micro-churches" in North Korea, where the team helped rescue more than 300 North Koreans. He was also the impetus behind the planting of the Every Nation church in Ulaanbaatar, Mongolia.

Today, there are more than 100 congregations in the United States, Asia, and Europe that can trace their beginnings back to the influence, missionary teams, or church planters from King's Park International Church. Many of those are second- and third-generation church plants. Recently, the King's Park leadership team realized that they had planted the first fourth-generation church—that is, Tom Jackson was sent from King's Park to plant the Every Nation church in Lviv, Ukraine, that birthed the church in Ternopil, Ukraine, that birthed the church in Torrevieja, Spain, along with outreaches in Paris and Venice. King's Park, the Every Nation church founded in Chapel Hill, North Carolina, continues going into all the world to make disciples, train leaders, and plant churches.

Every Nation—South Africa
Established 1988

I would say that Every Nation in South Africa is one of the most active church-planting centers—not just for our movement, but around the world today. If the goal is to plant churches that make disciples, train leaders, and (in short order) plant other churches throughout the region, what has been happening in Southern Africa is an excellent model. The names of cities in which Every Nation churches have been planted since 1988 are too numerous to mention. Primary church-planting centers for Every Nation in South Africa are located in Cape Town, George, Grahamstown, Johannesburg, Midrand, North/Kuils River, Potchefstroom, Stellenbosch, and Tshwane/Pretoria—all together establishing sixty new Every Nation churches and Every Nation Campus chapters. In addition to the church-planting initiatives in South Africa, teams from these churches have established new Every Nation churches in about ten other African nations, as well as beyond Africa, including the United Kingdom and Germany. New church plants are also in progress in Brazil, France, Mauritius, and Mozambique.

Every Nation churches in the region have embraced the vision of reaching every university campus. With Every Nation Campus chapters on twenty-nine regional campuses and over 6,000 students in campus groups, their mission is to expose every student on every campus to the gospel. In some locations, several of our churches work together on a particular Every Nation Campus chapter. To do this well, they have even upgraded their ministry school and have a consistent number of upcoming campus missionaries and church planters that are being trained.

Every Nation Church, London—London, United Kingdom
Established 1993

Wolfi Eckleben and his wife, Ali, were sent out from the His People Baxter Theatre congregation (now renamed Every Nation Baxter) on the University of Cape Town campus. Their objective was to start a church and campus ministry in London. They landed at Heathrow Airport with "two backpacks and a vision" for discipleship, campus ministry, equipping leaders, and planting churches. Having arrived full of faith and vision, they got to the end of their first year with only a handful of people joining the struggling church plant. Wolfi and Ali had expected so much more. They had left South Africa on one-year open-return air tickets, and the expiration date was quickly drawing near. Thankfully, they decided to tear up those return tickets and continue their efforts in London.

Within the first few weeks of that second year, their small flat was overflowing, and within two months they were renting a meeting room in one of the world's top universities, Imperial College London. It was an unprecedented turnaround, especially for church planters laboring in such a spiritually barren field. Even the Ecklebens could hardly believe it. Twenty years later, the Every Nation leadership team in London has listed over fifty people who have come through their church and gone on into some form of vocational ministry. It also played a key role in planting Every Nation churches in Belgium, France, Northern Ireland, Poland, and Spain, as well as planting two more congregations in London. The universities of Western Europe continue to be some of the most spiritually dark places in the world. However, Every Nation church-planting initiatives are moving forward with sustainable momentum.

Every Nation London has even planted a church in China. It's quite an extraordinary story. It started in a prayer meeting where a group was regularly praying for the nations, and some key leaders were stirred to go on a mission to China. During a time of praying in tongues, a certain word was being repeated over and over. The leadership team soon discovered that it was the name of a city in central China, and concluded that the Lord was leading them to a campus in that city. What followed was an intense seven-year period of mission initiatives. Over 150 people from London went on short-term trips to this city. A few of the leaders spent extended seasons training local leaders and overseeing the fledgling work. Many were saved and discipled, including a young couple that was eventually ordained as senior pastors when the church was launched. This same couple now serves on the leadership team of that region.

Victory—Dubai, United Arab Emirates
Established 1995

"Emirate" is an Arabic word describing a territory that is hereditary and ruled by a monarch or prince. Internationally recognized states with emirs as rulers have become rare, most being incorporated into more modern forms of government. The most notable exception is the United Arab Emirates (UAE), established in 1971 as a federation of seven emirates located on the eastern coast of the Arabian Peninsula. Dubai, the most populous city of the UAE, has grown steadily to become a global city, emerging as the business and cultural hub of the Middle East and the entire Persian Gulf. It has become a popular tourist destination and has a surprising level of religious freedom for a country ruled by Muslim emirs. Twenty-first-century Dubai is a key city from which Every Nation churches and campus ministries have been planted throughout the Middle East.

Our church was established in the Middle East when Victory Tarlac sent Pastor Rouel and Febs Asuncion to Dubai. Victory Dubai began with thirty-five members in 1995, mostly Filipino expatriates. In more than two decades, the church in Dubai grew to several thousand members, and it has been making disciples, training leaders, and planting other Every Nation churches throughout the Middle East, including the following cities. Several of these churches are second-generation church plants.

- ↗ 1999 — Sharjah, UAE

  Kuwait City, Kuwait
- ↗ 2000 — Tehran, Iran
- ↗ 2001 — Ras Al Khaimah, UAE
- ↗ 2005 — Doha, Qatar

  Mumbai, India
- ↗ 2008 — Abu Dhabi, UAE
- ↗ 2010 — Ajman, UAE (planted by the church in Sharjah)
- ↗ 2012 — Pune, India (planted by the church in Mumbai, which is also planting another church in New Delhi)
- ↗ 2013 — Al Ain in Abu Dhabi, UAE

  Colombo, Sri Lanka (planted by the church in Sharjah)
- ↗ 2015 — Sivas, Turkey (planted when persecution in Iran caused a number of Christian converts to flee, seeking asylum in Turkey)

  Yerevan, Armenia (planted by the church in Sharjah)
- ↗ 2016 — Kathmandu, Nepal (planted because of the large number of Nepalis in the Abu Dhabi congregation)

"Ask of me, and I will make the nations your heritage, and the ends of the earth your possession" (Psalm 2:8). The Hebrew word for nations refers to "Gentile or heathen nations," and the word for heritage implies "to take possession." We are not simply to ask for nations we like—those that are comfortable and convenient to go to. Part of our inheritance is asking the Lord for creative-access nations that are resistant to the gospel. Jesus did not send us on an impossible mission. He gave His disciples the power of the Holy Spirit and the assurance of His abiding presence. Some nations may require high-level creativity and supernaturally opened doors; that doesn't mean they are unreachable.

OUR CHURCH-PLANTING STRATEGY

In 2 Timothy 2:1,2, the Apostle Paul challenged Timothy to entrust the deposit he had received of God's Word to the generations to come: "You then, my child, be strengthened by the grace that is in Christ Jesus, and what you have heard from me in the presence of many witnesses entrust to faithful men, who will be able to teach others also." Four generations of discipleship are mentioned—Paul, Timothy, faithful men, and those they will teach. Below are a few of the things we are entrusting to faithful men and women so they can teach them to others.

Church-planting initiatives create space for the next generation of leaders. Churches that repeatedly plant other churches typically send out some of their best leaders. That process represents ongoing steps of faith because church-planting churches are helping with start-up costs, and they have to replace those key leaders for the local church to continue to be effective. Next-generation leaders emerge when there is room to grow. Churches that are top-heavy in leadership (especially paid-staff leadership) have a hard time empowering young leaders. It doesn't matter how well you train and equip people; if there are no leadership opportunities being created by expansion and reproduction, then there is no need, no vision, and no challenge that will cause others to step forward.

One of the characteristics of a healthy church is its ability to raise leaders from its own congregation. Repeatedly importing staff and leaders from other churches are quick fixes to immediate needs. However, importing leaders often reveals a far more fundamental issue: one or more elements of the discipleship journey (the 4Es) have probably broken down. Either the church is not effectively engaging culture and community, establishing biblical foundations, equipping believers with basic ministry skills, or empowering disciples to make disciples.

Managing church growth is like tending a vineyard. Ron Lewis has a unique perspective on church planting. He often speaks of the church as "the Lord's vineyard" and the "planting of the Lord" (Isaiah 5:1–7; Matthew 20:1–16). "And now, O inhabitants of Jerusalem and men of Judah, judge between me and my vineyard. What more was there to do for my vineyard, that I have not done in it? When I looked for it to yield grapes, why did it yield wild grapes?" (Isaiah 5:3,4). The New American Standard Bible translates the words as "good grapes" and "worthless ones." The difference between wild grapes and good ones is primarily the cultivation.

Without cultivation and pruning, grapevines grow abundantly, but their fruit is wild and worthless. Overgrown vines that have never been pruned are a lot like overgrown churches. They keep adding more and more members, building bigger and bigger churches, and becoming less and less effective at making disciples. There may have been a church plant or two along the way, but proportionate to their growing membership, they could have planted twenty more churches.

The process of managing a vineyard is often counterintuitive because the objective is not how large the vine grows, but the quantity and quality of the fruit it produces. Vines that are intentionally stressed by lack of water, regular pruning, or being planted in difficult places like rocky soil tend to produce better grapes. It seems that the constant stress causes the vine to go into survival mode. All its energy and effort are concentrated on reproduction—that is, producing fruit designed for the survival of the seed it surrounds.

Church growth is not simply about developing ways to attract more members; it should be about making more disciples, training more leaders, and reproducing itself in more church plants.

Church planters usually have to develop their own leadership teams. Ideally, church-planting missionaries will assemble a full team to go with them—people with complementary gifts serving as pastors, evangelists, campus missionaries, and administrators. That's ideal, but in reality, waiting for a fully developed and qualified leadership team could mean waiting forever. Very seldom do church planters go to foreign countries with a full complement of staff or volunteers. In those cases, they just have to do some intense equipping to raise leaders—a lot like the American team during the initial Victory church plant in Manila's U-Belt. The imminent departure of the sixty-five missionaries meant that if the church plant was to survive, very young and inexperienced disciples would have to quickly step into leadership roles. Not only did the missionaries know that, the young Filipinos knew it too. There was no question about whether there would be opportunities for emerging leadership. As Victory continues to plant new churches, there are ever-expanding opportunities for our upcoming leaders to serve and lead.

Individual callings don't always serve the organization's mission. Every Nation church-planting initiatives are more organic than mechanic in that we plan around individuals' callings to go to a specific nation. But that doesn't mean we randomly send missionaries into all the world wherever people see a need. We definitely respond to needs, but we are not primarily need-driven. We are mission-driven. As an organization, we are compelled to follow our corporate mission and calling.

Whenever we consider a church-planting endeavor or an outreach ministry, the questions we immediately need to answer are: "How close are we to the campus? What access do we have to the students?" And in the final analysis, "If we're not going to engage students as well as the community, why are we going?" We have longtime friends and church members who are definitely called to serve people and win souls for Christ, but their ministry objectives address needs of communities that are outside of Every Nation's mission. Though we celebrate and cheer for these ministries, we stay on course to fulfill our mission.

What you measure and monitor improves. Stories of large churches with large numbers attending can divert us from our mission. It's important to note that Every Nation measures the success of a church plant not by attendance or finances but by the health of the church. In other words:

↗ Is the church effectively engaging nonbelievers with the gospel, establishing biblical foundations, equipping members to minister, and empowering disciples to make disciples?

↗ Is the church on its way to becoming financially self-supporting?

↗ Is the church giving to missionary endeavors outside of its own church?

↗ Is the church growing and reproducing by making disciples?

↗ Is the church developing leaders from its own congregation?

↗ Does the church have a vision and commitment to plant new churches?

By those metrics, there are many small churches that are far more healthy than some megachurches.

A healthy church can easily become infected with viruses that diminish its effectiveness. Below is an account of one such infection in Victory Manila from the book *RUN: Endure the Pain, Keep the Faith, Finish Your Race* by Pastor Ferdie Cabiling, who now serves as one of Victory's bishops.

> ... in September 2009 ... We were all still feeling the excitement from the 25th anniversary celebration of Victory ... Two-dozen key leaders from Victory in Metro Manila were working on a strategic plan for future growth. Someone wrote a very big number on the board that represented our attendance goal for the next decade. Everyone took a deep breath and, with a growing sense of excitement, began to focus on the goal of more than doubling our current attendance.
>
> Pastor Steve, who was the president of Every Nation by then, was in that meeting. Though Pastor Steve was now President Steve, he hadn't changed his habit of equipping and empowering others to lead. He came determined, as usual, not to interfere but to let the Filipino team he had developed take the lead. However, he knew something was wrong, even though he couldn't put his finger on it. He later explained, "As we examined our numbers, all of which seemed to be growing, my eyes fell on one set of numbers that had flat-lined over the last four years (and was even showing hints of decline)."
>
> While church attendance was exploding, the number of Victory groups and the number of Victory group leaders were not. As our strategic planning group began to evaluate things more closely, we began to see leadership voids everywhere. The result was a radical renewal of our emphasis on Victory groups and developing Victory group leaders. We had gotten distracted by the momentum of our growth and had begun fixing our eyes on the growing church attendance, rather than making disciples and training leaders. In terms of the race that had been set before us at Victory, we were

running down a steep incline, gaining momentum, beginning to lose control, and forgetting to fix our focus on what Jesus had called us to do—make disciples.[1]

Immediately after that serious evaluation with Pastor Steve, we started refocusing on what is most important—the raising and equipping of Victory group leaders. At the time of the evaluation, the ratio between small group leaders and members was running as high as fifteen members to one Victory group leader. While we were growing in numbers, the gap of the ratio between members and Victory group leaders widened. In other words, we were growing faster than our ability to raise new small group leaders. The following year, we launched a campaign called "Just One." This was the start of what we now call our annual discipleship convergence. Every small group leader is encouraged to equip and empower another small group leader. The progress has become evident. We have started to lower the ratio to one leader for every ten members. By 2018, the number of Victory group leaders in Metro Manila had increased to 8,398.

Our strategic objective is to develop and empower local leadership teams. Every church plant, cultural setting, and church-planting team is unique. Consequently, every timetable is unique. Some church planters stay for a few years; others stay for a lifetime. Our experience in Manila was that Pastor Rice came for one month, and though he returns periodically, he moved on after that to reap from another field. In contrast, Pastor Steve came and served as the senior pastor for twenty-five years. The importance is not the length of a missionary's stay, but its character.

With every year they stayed in the Philippines, we have seen Pastor Steve and Deborah become more and more enculturated. They have honored God by honoring the people, culture, and history of the Philippines. They have never demonstrated an air of superiority. Instead, they have constantly believed in us and empowered us as next-generation leaders. And when the time came for Pastor Steve to serve as president of Every Nation, he turned the church over to the local leadership team he had developed.

How inappropriate, discouraging, and out-of-character it would have been to ask someone from outside the Philippines to serve as the senior leader of Victory! Regardless of whether the initial church planters stay a year or a lifetime, the objective is to transfer the leadership to a team of local leaders.

Our primary mission is to make disciples among nonbelievers. Our commitment to finding the lost was mentioned in the previous chapter, when Pastor Rice asked the Christians from visiting youth groups not to return. There may be people with a similar vision for evangelism, discipleship, campus ministry, and church planting who were called to join us. However, it is always better to build on our own foundation rather than that which has been laid by other churches with other missions. The point is that in planting churches, we are not simply looking for growth via transfer—Christians wanting to try out the latest church in the city. Better to grow slowly with new believers than deal with the problems that are the result of simply attracting people from other churches.

GLOBAL MISSIONS CHALLENGE

There are already a lot of challenges to the faith and vision of Every Nation church planters in this chapter. Stepping back to look at the big picture of our missions strategy, the essential challenge is to begin with the end in mind.

Wolfi and Ali Eckleben went from South Africa to London with a sense of mission—to make disciples, win students to Christ, train leaders, and plant churches. Since they had never been to London before and knew no one, they had a very slow start as church planters. (The full story of their first year was quite discouraging.) But they refused to give up on the dream and the vision. After persevering through a very difficult first year, they experienced a breakthrough that has resulted in great fruit on campuses and in nations across Europe and beyond.

There are lots of people around the world, missionaries and church planters included, who consider our mission idealistic, even unrealistic. They might say that students in the world's top universities are too hard to win, church-wide participation in making disciples is impossible, church planting in highly restrictive nations is strictly forbidden, and so on. Is the Every Nation mission that idealistic? You bet it is, and that's precisely my point. I would even press that point a little further—that missionary church planters should begin with a clearly defined vision of what evangelism, discipleship, and church planting would look like in the ideal expression of their church. Visionary leadership is not just promoting **ideas**; it's instilling, managing, and maintaining **ideals**. If we don't begin with the end in mind, we might end up settling for something far less than what God's grace would have enabled us to accomplish. Jesus told His disciples to lift their eyes (their vision) to see that the fields are white with harvest—to engage in the kind of visionary leadership that looks to God as the one who "calleth those things which be not as though they were" (Romans 4:17, KJV).

Chapter 4

The Great Co-Mission

The Bible is not the basis of missions; missions is the basis of the Bible.

—Dr. Ralph D. Winter
U.S. Center for World Mission

"As the Father has sent me, even so I am sending you." And when he had said this, he breathed on them and said to them, "Receive the Holy Spirit."

—John 20:21,22

MISSIO DEI IS A LATIN PHRASE which means "the mission of God." That mission finds its origins in the Father's eternal plan of redemption that has been progressively revealed throughout history. The sacrifices required for atonement in the Old Testament were a foreshadowing of the sacrifice of the Lamb of God on the cross. God's promise to Abram (Genesis 12:1–3; 15:5) was not only to bless him with descendants as numerous as the stars of heaven; it was that through his seed, which was Christ (Galatians 3:16–22, NIV), every nation of the earth would be blessed with the gift of righteousness—including the Gentile nations. It seems that God the Father has been on a singularly focused mission to redeem mankind from the very beginning.

Missio Dei, as a theological term, has a long history that can be traced at least as far back as Augustine of Hippo in the fourth century.[1] The thirteenth-century Christian scholar Thomas Aquinas was perhaps the first to describe the *missio Dei* as a reflection of God's triune nature (Father, Son, and Holy Spirit). The key passage that describes this Trinitarian understanding of the *missio Dei* is in the Gospel of John.[2]

> On the evening of that day, the first day of the week, the doors being locked where the disciples were for fear of the Jews, Jesus came and stood among them and said to them, "Peace be with you." When he

had said this, he showed them his hands and his side. Then the disciples were glad when they saw the Lord. Jesus said to them again, "Peace be with you. As the Father has sent me, even so I am sending you." And when he had said this, he breathed on them and said to them, "Receive the Holy Spirit."

—John 20:19–22

The Father sent the Son; the Son sent the Holy Spirit as a Helper to those whom the Son would send into all the world to preach the gospel and make disciples of all nations. Aquinas was saying that the essence of the divine nature is that of the "missionary God" who has progressively and relentlessly sent.

Missio Dei has become very much a part of the current language of missiology, particularly over the last fifty years. However, as more skeptical interpretations of Christian theology have emerged—most notably doubts about the incarnation, the divine inspiration of Scripture, and salvation by *sola gratia, sola fide,* and *sola Christus* (grace alone, faith alone, and Christ alone)—the understanding of *missio Dei* has changed as well.

Looking at how God's mission applies to us, the contention has always been whether we should be doing more gospel proclamation or gospel demonstration. I think the answer is both. Perhaps we would do better to think of the mission of God in terms of the great "co-mission"—a dual mission of reconciliation and compassion, of preaching the gospel and meeting physical needs among the hearers. Honor God by telling His story; demonstrate His love by helping those in need. How complicated can that be? As it turns out, departing and moving further and further away from "the simplicity that is in Christ" (2 Corinthians 11:3, KJV) causes that great co-mission to bog down in complication and controversy. How unfortunate that is, since the church has been so clearly commissioned to do both!

The general understanding is that the mission of God and the mission of the church are one and the same—the redemption of all who are called and given the grace to believe the Good News. "For God so loved the world, that he gave his only Son, that whoever believes in him should not perish but have eternal life. For God did not send his Son into the world to condemn the world, but in order that the world might be saved through him" (John 3:16,17). Our prime directive is evangelical—to preach the gospel consistently, intentionally, and unashamedly, resulting in personal transformation by the power of the Holy Spirit. As the Apostle Paul wrote: "For I am not ashamed of the gospel, for it is the power of God for salvation to everyone who believes . . ." (Romans 1:16). Though there are countless ministries that hold to orthodoxy while ignoring the poor and doing little to alleviate injustice, our commitment to preach the gospel does not negate the call to compassionately serve the widow, orphan, and alien.

Part of Every Nation's mission is to establish socially responsible churches and campus ministries. To paraphrase John 20:21, Jesus said, "As (in the same way) the Father has sent me (on His mission), even so I am sending you (to all the nations)." The manner and motivation of the Father sending the Son is because "God so loved the world" (John 3:16). That is why and how Jesus sends us as missionaries—motivated by love, committed to His mission, and filled with His power. Consequently, compassion ministries are integral to evangelism and the church-planting mission.

Here are a few examples of how Every Nation churches proclaim the gospel in the context of compassion ministries—or show compassion in the context of proclaiming the gospel.

Christian Rehabilitation Center in Ukraine

Oleg Savchak currently serves as the lead pastor of Love and Healing Church in Ternopil, Ukraine. This church was originally planted by Shumylo Anatoly in 1993. Like all Every Nation churches, their mission is to engage nonbelievers with the gospel, make disciples, and train leaders. One of the ways they do this is by helping Ukrainians who are in desperate situations due to drug addiction. In 2001, the church established the Christian Rehabilitation Center as an outreach to drug addicts, using a Bible-based Ten-Step program. The center was constructed with the help of church members, former drug dependents, and a partnership with the Every Nation Church in London. About 100 rehabilitants go through the program each year. Currently, eighty graduates have become church leaders who spend at least part of their time at the center helping others gain freedom from addiction. A vast majority of the graduates have been led to a saving knowledge of and a life-transforming experience with Christ and have taken significant steps in their discipleship journey. Many have been restored to their families. Forty of the graduates now have growing families. Love and Healing Church has now established a second rehabilitation center for women.

Prison Ministry in Australia

In March 2017, Lilian Su'a, a member of our Every Nation church in Brisbane, Australia, attended a camp for at-risk youth organized by MS61, which stands for "My Story inspired through Isaiah 61."

Isaiah writes in the first verse of chapter 61 (NASB):

> The Spirit of the Lord God is upon me,
> Because the Lord has anointed me
> To bring good news to the afflicted;
> He has sent me to bind up the brokenhearted,
> To proclaim liberty to captives
> And freedom to prisoners . . .

The objective of MS61 is for every inmate in prison to hear the gospel and find the hope that is in Jesus alone. The organizers invited some community partners to attend the youth camp. One of those who attended was the program officer for the remand prison in Wacol, who, after seeing how effective the MS61 program was for the youth, encouraged the organizers to do the same program for the men in prison. Since a remand prison is a facility for those awaiting trial or sentencing, these men were on the verge of beginning their prison sentence.

Being a woman, Lilian was quite hesitant in the beginning to do any type of prison ministry, especially in a men's prison. However, the program officer saw how effective she was among the youth and encouraged her to give it a try. With the support of Neli Atiga, senior pastor of Every Nation Brisbane, Lilian began visiting inmates at the men's remand prison.

In the first eighteen months, approximately 150 men completed the program, and many became believers. There have been at least eighty men on the waiting list for each semester of the program. Those that put their trust in Christ as their Lord and Savior have started small groups among fellow inmates using *ONE 2 ONE*. Two of those that have been released from the prison now attend Every Nation Brisbane and are part of discipleship groups.

Ministry to the Muslims in the Philippines

The Peace Project began as a simple outreach among Muslim students in 2014. Jonathan heads the Peace Project, which is supported by Victory Manila.

A missionary couple invited Jonathan and his team to interact with Muslims at a swimming event during *Eid'l Fitr*—a religious holiday that marks the end of Ramadan. Being very surprised at how open the students were to listening to Bible stories, they organized a visit to their community, where the team members met with students and their families. They were warmly welcomed into their homes, but couldn't help noticing how poor most of the families were. Many students had not finished college and could not find stable jobs.

Jonathan and his team addressed the need by giving them a small allowance to help with educational expenses. During their second meeting, they introduced the Allowance by Faith program. The team members had very limited resources themselves, but they were able to offer PHP 150 (USD 3) per person per week as educational assistance for students. As the number of Muslim students grew to about forty, they shifted their program from student educational assistance to teaching these students life skills and leadership principles. For the sake of transparency, they asked parents to allow their children to attend the activities and training in a public school in the community, as well as Bible study classes (*Kitab*) on Saturdays. And so a regular outreach to their community began.

When a Muslim teacher began to question their activities, they moved to another location within the same area. Because of this incident, the number of students dropped from forty-one to twelve. However, those twelve were the first to respond to the gospel and be baptized. From then on, the Lord has consistently guided the team in winning more Muslim men and women to become followers of Jesus Christ (*Isa al-Masih*).

By mid-2018, eighty-two Muslims had been baptized—seventy-seven students and five parents. Jonathan's team continues to give weekly allowances to selected students and offers trainings on how to become a godly influence and lead their community. They also started a monthly fellowship among the parents to build relationships and communicate the gospel to them. Recently, the parents who became followers of Jesus started a house church.

English with a Difference in Myanmar

In 2001, *Newsweek* described Myanmar as one of the worst nations where one can be a student. The military had just crushed student-led protests, and it had also shut down or limited the functions of many universities. Amidst this backdrop, in June 2001, Carlo and Sandra Ratilla moved to Yangon, Myanmar. They were sent from Victory Makati in Manila to birth a church among the Burmese youth. They immediately faced challenges in this Buddhist country that was run by a military dictator at that time. Local missionaries presented them with a list of dos and don'ts for life in their newly adopted country. The list was quite foreboding— the state listens in on phone calls, reads emails, follows missionaries. Bibles cannot be opened in public, and group gatherings of more than twelve young people are forbidden. Fear crept into their hearts, and by November, five months later, they were ready to give up on the mission. Then came a moment of inspiration from MTV, of all places.

Carlo began to see the impact MTV was having—the clothing, lifestyle, and values—as well as the influence of the drug lords on the youth of Myanmar. Carlo began to ask himself: *Why can't it be God's Word that has this impact on the next generation?* The mandate was straightforward— reach out to the youth of Myanmar with the gospel of Jesus Christ—but the method was the challenge. How does one reach out to the youth in such a highly restricted nation? It was time to go on the offensive—but very carefully. Any kind of "offensive" in Myanmar, especially one related to the student population, was particularly dangerous. The offensive needed to be tempered with wisdom and guidance from the Holy Spirit. In creative-access nations like Myanmar, it was necessary to think of new ways to engage students. This realization led to something they did not expect: filling the education vacuum and appealing to the national obsession to learn English. In May 2002, Carlo and Sandra established a program called "English with a Difference," also known as E++.

The E++ program was a combination of a church service and an English class. It wasn't simply an English tutorial class using the Bible as a text;

it was a church service. There was nothing covert or secretive about E++. Sunday after Sunday, they declared boldly that they were a church, teaching English and life skills based on the Bible. Young Buddhists who would not normally come to a Christian church came to E++. The results have been far greater than the Every Nation team in Myanmar could have expected. Hundreds of young people, including Buddhist monks, eventually attended every Sunday.

"This is a 'God-idea,'" exclaimed a visitor from America when she chanced upon their Sunday church service, held at the ballroom of Summit Parkview Hotel. Since starting their Sunday services (using the E++ format) in May 2002, they were able to meet boldly for three years without government interference. However, in September 2005, local authorities confronted the manager of Summit Parkview about the services, and the Sunday meetings were stopped. As a result, their Sunday services were relocated to what has now become the Every Nation Church Yangon. From an "English-education-Sunday-service," the meetings evolved into a full-blown bilingual Burmese and English church service by January 2006. Since then, they have added two more services, one of which is a purely Burmese service.

Global Disaster Relief

When disasters strike on local, national, and global levels, and particularly when Every Nation churches are affected, our churches in the region provide relief efforts. These include providing funds, supplies, and medical and relief operations—and in some cases reconstruction teams. That was the case with the devastating tsunami that hit Banda Aceh, Indonesia, in December 2004; the catastrophic Cyclone Nargis that hit Yangon, Myanmar, in May 2008; and the March 2011 earthquake and tsunami in Japan. More recently, Every Nation churches have been directly involved with relief efforts following the destructive April 2015 earthquake in Nepal; the August 2017 Typhoon Harvey floods in Houston, Texas; and in November 2013 with Typhoon Haiyan (locally known as Yolanda) in Leyte, Philippines. In the days and weeks following Haiyan, retired Colonel Dennis Isleta, who now serves as senior pastor at Victory Makati, gained permission to use military helicopters and coordinated a massive and combined relief effort from Victory and Operation Blessing. Eventually, medical teams made their way to Leyte. Generators and vans were also donated because the storm had totally destroyed the electrical power grid and most of the cars on the island. Later, Every Nation partnered with Habitat for Humanity to build scores of new homes for victims of the destructive storm surges.

Healing and Mercy Ministry in the United Arab Emirates

Currently, we have several Every Nation churches in the Middle East, including congregations in Bahrain, Iran, Kuwait, Oman, Qatar, Saudi Arabia, and the UAE. Many workers in the Middle East are victims of abuse from their employers. More than five million Filipinos are overseas contract workers, and over 60 percent of these live in the Middle East.

Because there are many incidents of such abuse, these contract workers often seek refuge. Every Nation churches in the UAE started the Healing and Mercy Ministry in 2012. The director, Ruth Barrios, established affiliations with the Overseas Workers Welfare Administration representative and began coordinating with the Philippine Consulate in Dubai. The Healing and Mercy Ministry mobilized staff members and volunteers to visit affected workers once a week for counseling and ministry—and to eventually preach the gospel to them. Filipinos who had been repatriated were channeled through various Every Nation churches. Part of their ministry is hospital visitation among these abused workers. Our staff and volunteers have received identification badges that have given them official access to the hospital, and have ministered to patients regardless of their nationality or religious backgrounds. They even had the opportunity to minister to three comatose patients. Doctors had given up hope for them, but as our team came in and started praying for them, all three came out of their comas. Two ended up serving in one of our churches in the UAE before they decided to go home and become members of our church in the Philippines.

Compassion Ministries across Every Nation

Johannesburg, South Africa—Our Every Nation churches in Johannesburg have different compassion ministry initiatives in their community. African Havens has helped over 240 babies find families. The Malibongwe Programme aims to help mothers start businesses by providing them with capital. Over 90 percent of the mothers supported by this program have been successful in starting their businesses. The Car

Guard Programme helps unemployed men by providing work for them on Sundays guarding cars. Through the program, many men come to the saving knowledge of Christ, have their dignity restored, are connected to a discipleship group, and are assisted in finding long-term employment.

Mumbai, India—For ten years in the slums of Mumbai, members of our church and students who are part of Every Nation Campus have been ministering to children who are born and live in the local brothels.

Fusagasugá, Colombia—Children's Net is a compassion ministry of our Every Nation church in Colombia. It is an outreach primarily to poor children ages six to fifteen years old. Around 150 to 200 children come for special events like Christmas. Although they have about 200 children in the loop, only around fifty to sixty of them come every week. Every Saturday, they teach Bible, art, and music classes. They also provide health workshops, hygiene kits, school supplies, and gifts on special occasions.

DISCIPLESHIP IS OUR PRIMARY MISSION

Planting disciple-making churches is the most important ministry of a church-planting organization. That would be true for any church or any kind of Christian movement. Among the hundreds of Every Nation church-planting initiatives going on all over the world, the examples provide practical insights into how the "socially responsible" part of the Every Nation mission is being applied.

Establish biblical foundations. In the parable of the seed and the soils, Jesus referred to seed that sprung up quickly but withered because it was not deeply planted. It is not enough to be enthusiastic about an organization's mission but neglect to build deep biblical foundations with an emphasis on reconciliation, forgiveness, and alleviating injustice. We can never be satisfied by merely providing for physical or social needs without preaching the gospel—or offering a drink of water to a thirsty person without also offering the living water by which that person will never thirst again (John 4:7–15).

The mission of God is redemption and salvation through faith in the atoning sacrifice of Christ. That's not the only concern of Every Nation churches, but it's our chief concern and our primary mission.

Successful church plants are the ones that are able to quickly establish positive momentum. Very seldom do churches that have been stagnant for years take off and begin to grow rapidly. The ability to successfully engage non-Christians and begin to make disciples in the early planting stages is the primary factor that creates that momentum. One of the characteristics of living organisms or organizations is that they grow as their cells multiply. Christian movements (whether they are planting churches, providing relief and development, or running education programs) tend to be unsustainable if there is not some kind of built-in multiplication factor.

Let's be very clear: there are indeed churches and organizations (secular and faith-based) that feel a definite call to those kinds of ongoing compassion ministries. However, Every Nation's mission is different. Our churches are established as we engage unbelievers with the gospel. We gain strength, momentum, and giving capacity as those disciples are equipped and empowered to make generation after generation of other disciples. At that point, our churches are able to fund compassion ministries on our own and even hire needed staff. We are, however, very intentional about planting the gospel in the hearts of people who become disciples and members of churches that eventually (often very quickly) become socially responsible congregations.

Discipleship and church planting begin with relationships. Our ministry philosophy is that effective discipleship is based on effective relationships. Consequently, we begin every church plant by engaging unbelievers in relationships that will lead to individual gospel presentation. Sometimes those interactions can be as simple as sharing a meal together, socializing over tea or coffee, playing Frisbee, badminton, board games, or any number of ways with which missionaries engage unbelievers. Our missionaries have to be very creative in this. Some activities even include giving guitar lessons or doing academic tutorials, giving tips on how to get better grades, or teaching leadership principles.

Though some of those activities do indeed meet social or economic needs, the clear objective should be to demonstrate and communicate the gospel, or these efforts may not bear fruit.

Because of our limited time and resources, we have to be focused and strategic, particularly in the early stages of growth. That is to say, we don't focus so much on random acts of kindness but on strategic or intentional acts of kindness—activities that open doors to engage people with the gospel and make disciples.

Each church figures out the local needs of its community. As president of Every Nation, someone once asked Pastor Steve, "Who is in charge of social responsibility for Every Nation?"

"Well, no one," he replied. "There is no department or director of social responsibility."

Since one question often begs another, he was ready for the follow up: "Then how is it that you intend to plant socially responsible churches and campus ministries?"

The simple answer is that each Every Nation church determines the pressing needs of its community and develops the most efficient and effective ways of addressing those needs. In other words, expressions of social responsibility to our communities are almost always localized endeavors and exist as initiatives of local believers and churches. Most of these Every Nation compassion initiatives result in strategic opportunities to preach the gospel and make disciples. However, some just show people that "God so loved the world" in their time of need. Strong churches and healthy disciples are able to respond to these local needs in their community.

Every Nation churches with the most effective compassion initiatives are those that have demonstrated a long-term commitment. Victory Pasig in Metro Manila was planted in 2000 with the purpose of reaching the students of Rizal High School, which at that time was listed in the Guiness Book of World Records as the largest high school in the world, with a population of more than 20,000 students. In 2003, Dr. Joey Castro, who served as the senior pastor of Victory Pasig, wanted to help kids in the community who couldn't afford to go to college after high school. He and his wife, Tess, who is also a medical doctor, helped one student enroll in college. Seeing hope and joy swell for this student and his family, they challenged the church to help send another student to school, then another. They shared the vision to more people who were also willing to help in this endeavor, and so were able to send more. They called this project the Life Scholarship Program.

Over the next four years, educational support for these few students expanded to cover fifty students and counting. Eventually, more and more members of the church joined Dr. Joey in his little initiative until there were just so many kids being sent to school and so many donors giving that, in 2007, some church leaders, with the help of very generous donors, decided to incorporate the Life Scholarship Program into what is now known as the Real LIFE Foundation.

To date, the Real LIFE Foundation has awarded more than 2,000 scholarships, costing around USD 1,200 per scholar per year. We have seen 416 Real LIFE Foundation-assisted students graduate from college. In 2015, Bishop Ferdie ran across the Philippines and raised over PHP 2,000,000 (USD 40,000) for Real LIFE Foundation scholars.

The point here is that while our church participates in many compassion initiatives, we major in only a few. We don't randomly scatter our involvement but focus on the compassion ministries we have been called to support. The result is that church members have a vested interest in these compassion ministries. Consequently, we are highly motivated to build upon those previous investments. By our concentrated efforts, our compassion ministries make a far greater impact than we could have accomplished with a less focused approach.

GLOBAL MISSIONS CHALLENGE

Every Nation pastors, missionaries, and church planters need to carefully think through each of the principles and priorities highlighted in this chapter.

First of all, with the pressing needs in the world today, compassion ministries might be considered the easiest thing in this world. To find places to serve or donate, all we have to do is take a quick look around. However, because there is so much that can be done, there are a few things that will require more prayer and leading by the Holy Spirit. We have to discover where, how, and when to invest our limited resources.

Secondly, our churches don't support political parties or positions. We understand our calling to be ambassadors and ministers of reconciliation. Jesus was a friend of sinners—all kinds of sinners, including tax collectors who enriched themselves by extortion, Samaritans with their skewed theology, and even religious leaders whom He so vigorously opposed for having corrupted Judaism. He offered pardon and reconciliation to them all. Jesus was even an advocate with the Father for the souls of those who crucified Him, saying, "Father, forgive them, for they do not know what they are doing" (Luke 23:34, NIV). As Christ's ambassadors, we are ministers of reconciliation with God to all peoples—regardless of their social or political affiliations.

Thirdly, Every Nation pastors and church planters need to be very clear about our calling. Jesus is the Advocate and Mediator between parties that seem to have broken and irreconcilable relationships. Fallen humanity is by nature full of enmity and self-righteousness; God by His nature is uncompromisingly righteous and infinitely holy. And yet we are reconciled to God by Jesus, who identified with and took up the causes of both as the Mediator between God and fallen humanity. Regardless of our individual callings, as Christians, we all have the responsibility of the ministry of reconciliation (2 Corinthians 5:17–21). As Jesus said to His disciples, "As the Father has sent me, even so I am sending you" (John 20:21).

2 MISSIONARY-SENDING MOVEMENTS

The spirit of Christ is the spirit of missions.
The nearer we get to Him, the more intensely
missionary we become.

— Henry Martyn
   Missionary to India and Persia

And this gospel of the kingdom will be
proclaimed throughout the whole world
as a testimony to all nations, and
then the end will come.

— Matthew 24:14

PART
TWO

THERE HAVE BEEN MANY GREAT SPIRITUAL AWAKENINGS throughout church history, and often those outpourings of the Holy Spirit have spread like fire through fields of dry brush. Among the more recent from the last few centuries are the British Evangelical Revival under the preaching of John Wesley and George Whitefield, and in America: the Great Awakenings of the eighteenth and nineteenth centuries, the Azusa Street Pentecostal revivals in the twentieth century, and the Charismatic movement of the 1960s and 1970s. The spiritual awakenings of the twenty-first century that are mostly taking place in the global South are so expansive that within a few decades the dominant centers of Christianity are likely to be in Africa, Asia, and Latin America.

FROM MOVEMENTS TO MISSIONS

Throughout the last twenty centuries, individual missionaries have gone into all the world to preach the gospel. However, movements that have attempted to systemically send hundreds and thousands of missionaries into all the world have been far less common. The focus of this book, and particularly this section (Chapters 5–8), are spiritual renewals that turned into worldwide missionary-sending movements. There have indeed been such movements throughout church history: the ancient Nestorian-founded churches of the far east, Patrick going to Ireland, William Carey in India, the Jesuits in every direction, and the churches in South Korea today—just to name a few. However, these long-term, systematic mission-ary-sending movements have been few and far between.

I have highlighted four missionary-sending movements in this book—the Jesus movement of the early church, the Moravian movement, the Student Volunteer Movement, and the current missionary-sending movement in the global South. Why these four? It's not that these are the greatest, most effective, or most geographically expansive—though they have all of those characteristics. I have highlighted these four because of lessons and potential applications to our own movement.

Chapter 5

Early Church Missionary-Sending Movement

The holy Apostles and disciples of our Saviour were scattered over the world.

—Eusebius Pamphili (AD 263–339)
Author, *Historia Ecclesiastica*

And he called the twelve together and gave them power and authority over all demons and to cure diseases, and he sent them out to proclaim the kingdom of God and to heal.

—Luke 9:1,2

MOST OF US HAVE A ROMANTICIZED UNDERSTANDING of the first-century church. We think about the spread of Christianity in the context of the early years in Jerusalem and missionary journeys of the Apostle Paul. That period is sometimes considered the high-water mark of Christianity, with everything since being on a downward trajectory with regard to power, purity, and influence. And yet nothing could be further from the truth.

Irrespective of the impact of the first-century apostles (the twelve, the seventy, and every other first-century disciple who went out proclaiming the good news), their efforts alone cannot account for the phenomenal growth of Christianity, particularly in the latter half of the third century—long after all the first-century apostles were dead. In AD 250, after over 220 years of evangelistic efforts, Christians made up only 1.9 percent of the Roman Empire—that is, one Christian for every fifty pagans. Fifty years later, in AD 300, Christians made up over 10 percent of the Empire—one Christian for every ten pagans.[1] This all took place before the Edict of Milan in AD 313, by which Christianity was granted toleration from persecution throughout the empire. The astounding growth in one or two generations begs the question: What was going on in the Christian world in the fifty years between AD 250 and 300? What can we learn from it? Do we have the courage, commitment, and clarity of mission to emulate their efforts?

LESSONS FROM THE EARLY CHRISTIAN MOVEMENT

There are so many things that can be learned from the first three centuries of the Christian movement, far too many for a single chapter. Below are a few takeaways for us.

1. Christianity spread as ordinary people told the story in ordinary ways. The gospel spread naturally through the first three centuries (AD 33–300). In the first few years, there were large crowds that gathered in and around the Temple—for example, on the Day of Pentecost and the public gatherings in Solomon's Portico. The missionary journey of the Apostle Paul also included stories of large public gatherings. However, outside of those early dramatic events, rarely were there large gatherings with the public preaching of the gospel. Most early Christians would never have seen anything remotely similar to a Billy Graham or Reinhard Bonnke evangelistic crusade of any size.

There were almost no church buildings for the first 150 years. Meetings were conducted "from house to house" (Acts 5:42) and in small groups.[2] There were no concise formulas or spiritual laws for salvation. The Christian faith was transmitted like the common cold, from person to person, as each tried to explain experiences of faith in his or her own way. Some learned about Christianity through friendships, stories of exorcisms or healing, or service as slaves and servants to Christians.[3] People throughout the Roman Empire and beyond were converted and churches formed in every way imaginable, and probably some ways that weren't. Without any precedents or strategic plan to follow, Christian missionaries were just ordinary people who were making it up as they went along. What held it all together was the common experience of the resurrected Christ.

Christian apologists began to emerge in the second century. We think of apologists as those who debate with unbelievers over the philosophical and scientific evidence for the faith. There was indeed some of that taking place. However, second-century apologetics was, more than anything else, simply an explanation of what Christians actually believed.

Robert L. Wilken, Professor of the History of Christianity emeritus at the University of Virginia, wrote:

> A lot of early apologetics was not defense but simple explanation. In his *First Apology*, Justin Martyr gave an account of Christian worship. He also talked about baptism. He didn't try only to establish a link to the larger culture or prove Christianity true. He also tried to tell people what Christians actually did in worship and what they believed. Today I believe the most significant apologetic task is simply to tell people what we believe and do.[4]

In the early third century, Hippolytus of Rome (AD 170–235) described the classes which led to baptism. Skilled teachers engaged inquirers in dialogues designed to point the way to conversion. As twenty-first-century Christians have become more formal and methodical in our evangelistic presentations, we tend to sound more mechanical and, unfortunately, less sincere. In other words, we may be talking at people rather than with them. We're not as good at listening or as comfortable with evangelistic dialogues that tend to wander off-script. Ordinary people from our Every Nation church in Madrid did one ordinary thing—listening—that led to people coming to Christ.

Every Nation in Madrid

Over the years since our Every Nation church in Madrid was planted, Mel and Tanya Calingo, Elmer and Joy Matienzo, and other team members have focused on relational evangelism when engaging all kinds of nonbelievers. One crucial lesson the Madrid team has learned is the art of listening. If our team members do all the talking (talking **at** rather than talking **with** people), they will forfeit their right to be heard.

Recently, our church in Madrid has been equipping believers to minister and reach out to people they haven't even met. Many of these are what we would call first-contact nonbelievers. In other words, they are hearing the gospel for the first time and have little or no exposure to the Bible. Once relationships are established, those reaching out use a tool like

THEGODTEST as an opener for conversations. They then transition by sharing their personal testimonies and relating them to real life. Depending on their degree of openness, they start to communicate the gospel by illustrating how Christ bridged the gap between God and mankind. They try not to rush through these conversations and avoid any kind of argument. At the end of each conversation, whether or not a person chooses to take a step toward following Christ, the vast majority would never refuse an offer for prayer. Of course, our missionaries pray for them on the spot, another first-time experience for them.

There was one incident in which team members had done *THEGODTEST* with two young women. The young women happened to walk by as the team was sharing with a few other people and interrupted the conversation to say, "You have to listen to these guys. Their message can change your life." These two women had not accepted Christ as Lord and Savior, but their hearts had been moved as our missionaries listened to, encouraged, and prayed for them.

Week after week, the team goes to the same plaza near the largest university campuses in Madrid to engage in meaningful and thoughtful conversations with individuals and groups. Sometimes they run into the same people, and they're always happy to see them. One man, Eduardo, after having been engaged in several conversations about the gospel in the plaza, gave his heart to Christ and is now going through *ONE 2 ONE*. He is one of the upcoming leaders being trained in the church.

2. The first-generation apostles not only went to preach the gospel, they also kept going. Jesus said to His disciples, "Go therefore and make disciples of all nations, baptizing them in the name of the Father and of the Son and of the Holy Spirit" (Matthew 28:19). William Carey's famous treatise on the church's missionary responsibility initially received a lot of theological criticism. Local ministers in his day were uncomfortable with the idea of being obligated to go to nations and make disciples of people groups they considered uncivilized. As silly as it sounds, those who didn't like the idea of the Great Commission as an imperative made their case by questioning the literal meaning of the word "go." Many are still making that same assertion. D.A. Carson in his commentary on Matthew writes:

> Only the context can decide the question. While it remains true to say that the main imperatival force rests with "make disciples," not

with "go," in a context that demands that this ministry extend to "all nations," it is difficult to believe that "go" has no imperatival force.[5]

The meaning of the passage (from both the context and literal translation) is not to simply go on a single mission trip but "as you continue going to all nations, continue making disciples."

That idea was exemplified by Philip's missionary venture into Samaria. Philip, one of the seventy disciples, went to Samaria and preached the gospel with signs and wonders. As a result, a great number of the Samaritans believed and were baptized, including Simon the Magician (Acts 8:4–25). The evangelistic movement was so powerful and so fruitful that Peter and John came to Samaria. What followed was a subsequent Pentecostal outpouring as the apostles laid hands on the Samaritans, praying for them to receive the Holy Spirit. Afterward, Peter and John returned to the movement in Jerusalem, while Philip remained in Samaria.

At the height of the great Samaritan movement with all kinds of accompanying signs and wonders, an angel called Philip to leave. "Rise and go toward the south to the road that goes down from Jerusalem to Gaza," the angel instructed. Philip could have objected, "Hey, don't you realize what's going on here? The Holy Spirit is really moving among these Samaritans." Then again, when an angel appears and sends you to another mission field, you'd better go—even if that field is a desert.

In the world of Christian missions, there are two groups—those who venture out as pioneers and those who (after having gone out) become settlers. No matter how often I see it happen, I am still amazed at the faith and fresh commitment of those who feel called to go and go and go—those who have planted successful churches, yet answer the calling of the Holy Spirit to go out for the sake of Jesus, to start all over again. It would be so much easier to become missionary settlers with lots of finances, facilities, and adoring fans in their established congregations.

Here are just a few:

- ↗ Tom and Jean Jackson began making trips to Lviv, Ukraine, in 1990, and helped plant a church in 1992. In 2005, they became church planters again in Scotland.

- ↗ Gio and Mariel Saynes were sent out in 1997 to plant an Every Nation church in southwest China. Two years later, they moved again to plant a church in the southeast, which is now a thriving church. This church recently started their fifth congregation. In 2010, they were sent to plant Every Nation Macau, where they now oversee two churches.

- ↗ Russ and Debbie Austin left Mid-Cities Community Church in Midland, Texas, to plant SouthPoint Community Church in Jacksonville, Florida, in 1999.

- ↗ Jonas Bernales felt the Lord impress upon his heart to go to Bangkok, Thailand, in 2001. I was a little shocked when Jonas announced his plans to leave behind an established ministry as a senior pastor overseeing four churches in Dagupan City, Philippines, and move with his wife, Janice, and three children in order to plant a church in Bangkok. His labor has led to the planting of three more churches in Thailand.

- ↗ After September 11, 2001, Ron Lewis, while based out of King's Park International Church, cofounded and became a pastor of Every Nation New York City.

- ↗ Rey and Menchie Corpuz left Victory U-Belt and became church planters in Istanbul, Turkey, in 2005, and again in 2008 in Abu Dhabi, where Rey now oversees eight congregations, including a Nepali service and two other church plants in the emirate.

- ↗ Gareth and Taryn Lowe left Every Nation Grahamstown, South Africa, in 2007 and became church planters in Berlin, Germany.

- ↗ Dr. Joey Castro and his wife, Tess, left Victory Pasig in 2010 to become missionaries to Brunei.

↗ Gilbert and Shirley Naron left Victory Dasmariñas with their four children to become missionaries to Timor-Leste in 2013.

↗ Robert Hern was serving as a senior pastor in Victory Pioneer, a congregation of over 8,000 members in Mandaluyong City, Philippines. In 2015, he left with his wife, Jennifer, and two children to start a new church in San Diego, California. After a little over a year, the church in San Diego helped plant another church in Pasadena, California.

These are just a few examples of Every Nation pastors who left established and growing congregations to start over, go into all the world, and plant a new church. The travel logs of the original apostles, including the Apostle Paul, suggest that these men were not only willing to go and plant churches, but to move on to other cities and regions when those churches were established. Every pastor and former church planter has to continually ask themselves, *Am I willing to go again? Do I still have the faith and passion to pioneer a new church, a new movement in another city? Is my prayer still, "Here I am, Lord. Send me!"?*

3. Some flee opposition; others run toward it. Stephen, one of the seven deacons, was stoned to death by a mob enraged at his preaching. Those in the mob had "laid down their garments at the feet of a young man named Saul" (Acts 7:58).

> And there arose on that day a great persecution against the church in Jerusalem, and they were all scattered throughout the regions of Judea and Samaria, except the apostles. Devout men buried Stephen and made great lamentation over him. But Saul was ravaging the church, and entering house after house, he dragged off men and women and committed them to prison. Now those who were scattered went about preaching the word. Philip went down to the city of Samaria and proclaimed to them the Christ.
>
> —Acts 8:1–5

And that is how and why Philip came to Samaria; he was running away from Saul's persecution.

If you read Stephen's sermon in Acts 7, his message was true and to the point. However, it's hard to imagine what more he could have said to provoke the Jews into stoning him. There was definitely no "flee" in Stephen. Yet that was precisely what Philip did, and he was not alone. Those who fled from Saul also included some who "traveled as far as Phoenicia and Cyprus and Antioch, speaking the word to no one except Jews. But there were some of them, men of Cyprus and Cyrene, who on coming to Antioch spoke to the Hellenists also, preaching the Lord Jesus" (Acts 11:19,20). And so, the outpouring of the Holy Spirit in Samaria, the planting of the church in Antioch, and surely many other instances of the spreading of the gospel were the results of believers fleeing persecution.

Fleeing China

KC, Hope, and their family first moved to southwest China in 1998 to plant a church right after their missionary training at the Every Nation Leadership Institute's School of World Missions. In 2000, the police raided one of their meetings and detained seventy-five people for four hours. They could easily have been taken into custody, but thousands were praying, and they were inexplicably released before midnight.

Despite the persecution, the congregation grew even more. They changed the meeting place; KC even moved to a rural area and told the congregation of new believers, "I don't know when I'll have to leave, so you all need to rise up." They felt the same urgency to grow up quickly as we did back in 1984 in Manila—but no one was threatening us with arrest or imprisonment. Nonetheless, the young believers in China responded.

In 2002, about 200 armed police raided their meeting place again, and the wife of a local pastor was interrogated by the police for more than three hours. When she was asked how she became a Christian, she boldly shared her testimony and how God healed her from cancer. She even ended up inviting the police to church.

By God's grace, KC and Hope were not present at that meeting. With no time to return home, they fled with their two young sons to Hong Kong. Three weeks later, they landed in Shanghai to start over from scratch, knowing that their every move was being monitored. In spite of that, they were able to plant another church there. Eventually, they were warned to leave, under threat of arrest. They fled once more to Hong Kong and planted yet another church, but were forced to leave again when their visas would not be renewed. Eventually, the Lord led them back to

Taiwan, their home nation, where they started Every Nation Taipei in 2009. The eight churches KC and Hope planted continue to win people to Christ, make disciples, and train leaders.

Fleeing Kathmandu

Just recently, our missionaries who had served in Nepal for nine years got a visit from immigration authorities. After three weeks of official investigation by the immigration department, they were charged with proselytism and misuse of visa, and were given ten days to leave the country. For several days, our missionaries David and Esther were on the front pages of the newspapers and online news in Nepal.

Although they already had a plan to transition the leadership of the church within the next two years to the Nepali pastors who were studying in the School of World Missions in Manila, the situation forced them to make the transition immediate. David and Esther were then deported. In spite of this, the brand-new leadership felt led by the Holy Spirit to move forward and continue what the previous missionaries had started.

They now have a thriving church, and twelve new disciples were baptized in water in 2018.

Running into the Fire

When a house is on fire, the primary objective is to get everyone out safely. However, there are those who are called and equipped to run into the fire to fight it. That was the kind of thing that must have been going through the mind of the Apostle Paul as he was planting the church in Ephesus (Acts 19). He spent three years in Ephesus, and during those years (circa AD 55–58) there was no shortage of political, economic, and social conflict. That included book burnings, wild accusations, beatings, a disruption of commercial trade of idols, and a Jewish exorcist fleeing naked after being overpowered by a demoniac. At one point, the whole city gathered in the arena and descended into a kind of mass hysteria that almost turned into a riot. They dragged two of Paul's companions into the arena and worked themselves into a frenzy by shouting nonstop for two hours, "Great is Artemis of the Ephesians!" Paul himself was intent on going into that theater to address the enraged crowd, and was only restrained by his own followers. Paul was not one given to fleeing, but running into the fire to fight it.

Running into Mindanao

In May 2017, war broke out between Philippine government forces and Muslim extremists. The Peace Project team, led by Jonathan, saw the war as an opportunity to bring the love of God to the Muslim people. While it seems logical to stay away from these dangerous conflict areas, our team felt strongly that they must go right to the center of where the action was—to run into the fire. They immediately mobilized volunteers, sent out relief teams to three nearby cities where evacuees had fled, and coordinated their relief efforts with the local Muslim communities. One Muslim leader commented, "If all Christians were like you, there would be no terrorists in this country." As a result of these acts of compassion combined with proclaiming the love of God, 483 evacuees believed the gospel, including 120 members of Muslim families. The team also equipped and mobilized eighty-seven workers from three Every Nation churches to help the new believers get established and continue in their discipleship journey. In this instance, running into the fire produced results that were so overwhelming that they started another work in that city and another nearby one to bring Jesus Christ (*Isa al-Masih*) to the Muslim peoples.

Nowhere to Flee

In February 2018, a new religious law was passed in China that practically prohibited any unregistered church from operating. This was partly due to the government's concern that the number of Christians in China had outgrown the number of communist party members, and that the majority of those turning to Christ were young people. The new religious law was so extensive and discriminating to the underground church that many were immediately shut down, including a few of ours. Many more churches are currently undergoing harassment and intimidation from the authorities. One local policeman who knew about our existence in the city and with whom we have developed some goodwill said, "Honestly, we don't even know how to enforce this new religious policy." But our churches never backed down. For every congregation closed, more small group meetings are started everywhere in the city. They're determined to stand their ground until the government shuts them all down. The

Chinese believers reasoned, "Where else can we go? This is our city, and there is no place to which we can flee. We trust God to be our refuge."

4. The first-generation apostles planted the seeds that in time changed the world. However, in many cases the full impact of the seeds they planted would not be seen or appreciated for hundreds of years. Philip's mission to the desert place became quite fruitful. You've probably read the story. On the road to Gaza he met a court official of Candace, queen of the Ethiopians, and engaged him in a discussion about Jesus (Acts 8:26–39). The Ethiopian became a believer and was baptized on the spot. It is believed that millions of Ethiopian Orthodox Christians can trace the roots of their faith in Jesus Christ to that one convert.

Many Every Nation missionaries have experienced a harvest that is plentiful and ready for reaping. However, some have labored amidst intense opposition that is by nature financial, physical, and spiritual. Philip probably never knew about the impact of his brief encounter with the Ethiopian official. However, 2,000 years later, they're still celebrating his willingness to leave the Samaritan movement and go down to Gaza road.

Every Nation churches and campus ministries have only been in existence for a few decades. Consequently, we don't have examples like Philip and the thousand-year impact on millions of Ethiopian Christians, or of Saint Mark, traditionally known as the founder of the Coptic Church in North Africa. However, within a much shorter time frame, we know of many examples of faithful and fruitful small group leaders who are making a few disciples at a time. We need to celebrate and honor these small group leaders as those who are doing the essential work of the Great Commission—making disciples.

5. The Christian movement did not spread because it was easy to join. It was, in fact, just the opposite. From the Greek word *catechesis* we get the English word catechism. It means "the instruction." Those who had been instructed were said to have been catechized.

In the third century, Hippolytus wrote in *The Apostolic Tradition* (also known as the *Egyptian Church Order*) that "teachers were to examine candidates about their lives and their reason for embracing the faith."[6] In the fourth century, Augustine of Hippo outlined a similar procedure. After scrutinizing the candidate's motives, the catechist (instructor) would present the message of salvation history, from creation to the Second Coming.

The catechetical process was similar to what we would refer to as a new-believers class but only in concept, not in the commitment required. It sometimes took several years to complete, the goal being to ensure that hearers were sincere and that they had an authentic experience with Christ. Times of persecution made it crucial for churches to know whether or not people actually wanted to become Christian.

I'm neither suggesting nor discouraging a two- or three-year new-believers class. It all depends upon the cultural and religious context of the church. Our philosophy of leadership development is to give disciples the doctrinal foundation and training required to simply take their next step of faith as followers of Christ. Within a few months of being saved and filled with the Holy Spirit, new believers at Victory, for example, are typically leading or coleading a small discipleship group. Eventually, small group leaders will join a *Making Disciples* class. Many of those will go on to participate in short-term mission trips, and a handful might even enter full-time ministry and be trained using Every Nation's minimum global theological standard, known as *Leadership 215*. Some will continue by pursuing formalized seminary training. The discipleship journey should continually alternate between learning and doing. The idea of equipping for just the next step can be contrasted with a more traditional strategy—three to six years of theological training followed by a job search, which is often unsuccessful.

Jesus' model of discipleship was much more practical and effective. He would teach His disciples, then send them out; teach them some more, and send them out again. There are several recorded examples of this kind of discipleship. Training, followed by the steps of faith in action, probably happened many more times than recorded in Scripture. The disciples learned by stepping out in faith, putting the teaching of Jesus into practice. They were growing as they were going.

GLOBAL MISSIONS CHALLENGE

The early spread of the Christian movement was far more organic than systematic. Some went intentionally on missionary journeys. Others spread the good news along merchant routes throughout the Roman Empire and all the way to the Far East. Still others spread it during the first three centuries as believers fleeing from periodic persecutions. The challenge for us in the twenty-first century is to hold loosely our preconceived formulas of how the gospel spreads, how we can engage nonbelievers, and how churches are established. We're not following a formula; we're following the Holy Spirit. And as Jesus said in His encounter with Nicodemus, "The wind blows where it wishes, and you hear its sound, but you do not know where it comes from or where it goes. So it is with everyone who is born of the Spirit" (John 3:8).

So, in a sense, we may not know where we are going or what we are doing. This is because we recognize that the Holy Spirit sometimes leads and directs in ways that are counterintuitive. After all, we cannot completely understand His ways. While all heroes of the faith (Hebrews 11) and those in the first-century church were characterized by taking courageous stands, the Spirit led Philip to flee to Samaria (Acts 8:5), and an angel instructed him to abandon such a great harvest of Samaritans in order to present the gospel to a single Ethiopian in the desert. And for some reason, so many believers were drawn to Antioch. The Apostle Paul on his second missionary journey had fully intended to go to Bithynia, but "the Spirit of Jesus did not allow them" (Acts 16:7).

How locked in are you to the normal way things happen? How sensitive are you to the unexpected ways the Holy Spirit leads? Our strategic plans and church-planting initiatives need to be on the altar, lest we become like those who forge ahead on their own initiative rather than those who wait upon the Lord in prayer for direction.

Chapter 6

Moravian Missionary-Sending Movement

I have but one passion—it is He, it is He alone. The world is the field and the field is the world; and henceforth that country shall be my home where I can be most used in winning souls for Christ.

—Count Ludwig von Zinzendorf
Founder, the Moravian Church

Therefore, brethren, be all the more diligent to make certain about His calling and choosing you . . .

—2 Peter 1:10 (NASB)

ON AUGUST 13, 1727, a group of about 300 refugees who had fled from religious persecution gathered together in the makeshift commune that had been established for them near the southeastern border of modern-day Germany. The Roman Catholic Church had condemned them all as Protestants, excommunicates, and heretics. Among them were Lutherans, Separatists, Dutch Reformed, Anabaptists, Pietists, and even some reformed Catholics. For the previous four years, these refugees had been streaming into the little enclave on the farm of a benevolent nobleman. The meeting that Sunday was for prayer and the celebration of the Lord's Supper.

It was an unlikely collection of languages and allegiances as well as a mixed brew of religious passions. We twenty-first century Christians have a hard time understanding the theological intolerances of Christians in the late Middle Ages. In our minds, great opposition from the outside forces us to congregate around our common beliefs—atonement, the

Resurrection, the Lordship of Jesus Christ, and the hope of eternal life. However, most of these believers had been meeting in secret for all their lives, fearing arrest for their respective expressions of Protestantism. Consequently, they were not so quick to abandon the convictions for which they had so long suffered merely for the sake of Christian unity. Having found a refuge from their common persecutor, it wasn't long before they began to turn their intolerances upon each other. They would have done well to consider more carefully the exhortation of the Apostle Paul to the quarrelling members of the church in Corinth, "For while there is jealousy and strife among you, are you not of the flesh and behaving only in a human way? For when one says, 'I follow Paul,' and another, 'I follow Apollos,' are you not being merely human?" (1 Corinthians 3:3,4)

A few years into this endeavor, their like-minded benefactor—a member of the Austrian nobility, a devout Christian, and the owner of the estate—inserted himself into the situation. Count Ludwig von Zinzendorf moved from his own house into the camp of disputing factions and went to work. He set up rules of order for the governing of a Christian community. He also divided the community into small groups of two or three that met regularly for prayer, confession, and Bible study—discipleship groups or small groups, you might call them. Gradually, the passionate convictions among the Herrnhut community became singularly focused on honoring Christ though their worship, service, and surrender. And so, throughout the summer of 1727, there was a growing sense of spiritual expectancy.

At the Sunday service on August 13, as they were celebrating the Lord's Supper, the Moravian refugees experienced what could only be called a Pentecostal outpouring of the Holy Spirit. Their hearts were set on fire as the participants were all filled with the Spirit. Those who were not yet converted immediately accepted Christ as their Lord and Savior. There was an overwhelming sense of the presence of the Holy Spirit, evidenced by a general conviction of sin, the burning love for Christ and for one another, and the manifestation of the gifts of the Spirit. Members continued to meet in their small groups, confessing their sins and praying for individuals to be healed of infirmities. The renewal that continued through the next four months came to be known among the Moravians as the Golden Summer of 1727.

On August 27, two weeks after the initial outpouring of the Spirit, twenty-four men and twenty-four women pledged to spend one hour each day in round-the-clock prayer. Others joined in the daily intercession, and over the following decades, one generation after another enlisted in the 24/7 scheduled intercession that continued uninterrupted for over 100 years.[1]

Four years later, in 1731, Zinzendorf was inspired by a chance meeting at the coronation of King Christian VI of Denmark. Anthony Ulrich, an escaped slave from a sugar plantation in the West Indies, shared his story with the count. It turned out to be a divine encounter that would bear fruit a hundredfold and more. Zinzendorf brought Ulrich to Herrnhut to appeal for help for his enslaved countrymen.

Within six months, the Moravians' passion for Christ and commitment to prayer found its expression in their willingness to go. David Nitschmann (a carpenter) and twenty-five-year old Leonard Dober (a potter) volunteered to go as the first Moravian missionaries to the West Indies. After a season of prayer, the Herrnhut community sent out the two, who made their way to Copenhagen, Denmark—one step of faith after another. With a total of thirty shillings between them, they began to pray for means of transportation to the New World. There was no support, either financially or in any other way. Everyone thought they were crazy and predicted both would be dead in six months. C.G.A. Oldendorp recounted the opposition these missionaries faced in and along the way to Copenhagen.[2]

David Nitschmann and Leonard Dober eventually found their way to the West Indies, arriving on the island of St. Thomas in December 1732. They were the first wave of missionaries that would continue to be sent out from Herrnhut for decades. The following year, three more Moravian missionaries arrived in Greenland. In 1734, Moravians went to Lapland and Georgia; 1735, to Surinam; 1736, to Africa's Guinea Coast; 1737, to South Africa; 1738, to Amsterdam's Jewish quarter; 1739, to Algeria; 1740, to North American Indians and to Ceylon, Romania, and Constantinople. The years 1732–42 are unmatched when it comes to the history of Christian missionaries. Out of a Moravian community of 600, over seventy had gone on missions by 1742. By 1760, no fewer than 226 missionaries had been sent out from Herrnhut.

LESSONS FROM THE MORAVIANS AT HERRNHUT

It's difficult to extract meaningful takeaways from movements that occurred almost 300 years ago. Our world is far more different than what those who lived in the mid-eighteenth century could have ever imagined. But here are a few inescapable realities from the Moravians' example:

In the 1700s, going as missionaries into all the world (or any of the world, for that matter) was unprecedented. As impressive as the Moravians' 100-year prayer watch was, equally significant (or perhaps even more) was that their commitment to **pray** was combined with their willingness to **go**. Consider the historical context: the numerical expansion of Christianity had stalled by the end of the fifth century, and the percentage of Christians worldwide did not increase significantly for the next thousand years.[3] The churches of Asia Minor, North Africa, and the Far East had been all but persecuted into extinction by the 1200s. There had been no thought of international missions in the 200 years since the birth of the Protestant Reformation. Christendom, at least the Protestant expression of it, had fortified itself within the boundaries of Europe. The Moravians had no history or tradition of international missions to follow. There was almost universal opposition to missions outside the church's European footprint. Not surprisingly, the Moravian passion for missions was a model for those who would eventually follow. By the time of William Carey 150 years later, 2,158 Moravians had already answered the call to serve overseas. In the next 150 years, during the height of the Modern Missions Movement (1750–1900) and other similar movements around the world, the percent of the world population identified as Christian grew from 22 to 35 percent. That's what happens when Christians go into all the world preaching the gospel.

The perseverance of Moravian missionaries paid off. The proposed venture of the two Moravian missionaries was universally criticized and condemned by all in Copenhagen. Yet they persisted in their vision and the convictions about their own calling for almost five years, with hardly a word of encouragement from anyone to whom they appealed. Not only was there no precedent for evangelical international missions, there was no tradition of people giving support to foreign missionaries. Even if they had possessed the funds, no ship captain would agree to transport them on such a fool's errand. The difficulty of raising funds was as unprecedented as the mission they were attempting. At one point,

Leonard Dober declared that he would sell himself into slavery if that's what it would take for him to obtain passage to the West Indies.

There's no evidence that Dober actually came to that point, but their persistence did eventually pay off. Two court chaplains, the Reverend Reuss and the Reverend Blum, were finally convinced by their persistence that the two Moravians were indeed called by God, and the two ministers intended to support them fully. Other prominent individuals and government leaders in Copenhagen came to the same conclusion. Their passion even reached the royal court, where the queen graciously encouraged them and Princess Charlotte Amelia contributed funds for the journey. An officer of the court, Conrad Friedrich Martine, found a Dutch ship that would allow them to work as carpenters for passage to St. Thomas. And so, with a financial team in place, on October 8, 1732, they boarded a ship to the West Indies to begin making disciples of the nations.[4]

The Moravian global missions movement was one of the few times since the early church and the original apostles when the entire church felt the responsibility of the Great Commission. Moravian mission initiatives were not relegated to societies, associations, or interest groups within the congregation. Rather, everyone participated in the praying, the giving, and the going. If not one of the first times, it was perhaps the most notable and most influential. The Moravian missionaries made a deep impact on John Wesley and the Methodist movement, as well as William Carey and the Modern Missions Movement. In Chapter 10, I will further illustrate how imparting and sustaining the vision for world missions will change the world and change your church in ways that seem impossible.

The Moravians' discipline of devotional prayer was expressed in their sensitivity to the Holy Spirit and their willingness to surrender to His calling. Continual surrender that comes from prayer and a relationship with God is the key issue here. It seems as if the prayer and passion of each member of the Moravian community was like that of Isaiah. He too had experienced a divine encounter with God, and when the Lord asked, "Whom shall I send, and who will go for us?" Isaiah replied, "Here I am! Send me" (Isaiah 6:8). Apparently, that was a consistent prayer at Herrnhut—*Here I am. Send me!* Bishop Ferdie put it this way in his book, *Run*: ". . . your dreams and your vision could be, and probably are, far too small. God sees you with eyes of faith—what you could do and be with the power of the Holy Spirit. Remember, surrendering to God's calling will accomplish more for Christ's kingdom than all the dreams and visions we can conjure up on our own."[5]

The Moravians' persistence in prayer, worship, and surrender to going into all the world to make disciples represented a significant change for Reformed and Evangelical churches worldwide. Count Ludwig von Zinzendorf became renowned as "the noble Jesus freak" of the eighteenth century.[6]

CLARITY ABOUT OUR CALLING

A clear sense of calling enables us to persevere in the face of overwhelming obstacles. At the same time, uncertainty of our calling is among the primary targets of our adversary. Usually, the challenge to our calling as missionaries comes at us like a barrage of fiery darts. But those attacks are often held in reserve until a weakness in our confidence is revealed—when ministry partners are hard to find or when finances dry up; when we're threatened by spiritual or physical attack; when tragedy narrowly misses, or when it makes a direct hit. In the midst of those situations, with what degree of certainty and tenacity will we hold on to God's calling?

The Apostle Peter wrote, "Therefore, brethren, be all the more diligent to make certain about His calling and choosing you" (2 Peter 1:10, NASB). To be quite honest, it seems a lot easier for Peter, or one of the original apostles, to recommend being certain about such things. Jesus Himself had invited each of them to be His disciples. Then there was the Apostle Paul, who was called in a life-changing encounter with the resurrected Christ on the road to Damascus. Moses had his own encounter and calling by a voice coming from a burning bush.

How about your sense of calling?

"Not nearly so dramatic," you would probably say.

Possibly, you're not quite so certain either.

When I talk to individuals or groups about surrendering to God's calling to go into all the world, my emphasis is always on continuing in prayer until you are confident that it's really the Holy Spirit speaking to you—not just a mission of your own making. At the same time, I also understand that just more time in prayer won't automatically create certainty in your heart. Jesus answered a group of skeptical Jews in the Temple by saying, "My teaching is not Mine, but His who sent Me. If anyone is willing to do His will, he will know of the teaching, whether it is of God or whether I speak from Myself" (John 7:16,17, NASB). There's something about a willing and surrendered heart that seems to be a prerequisite to hearing God's calling with confidence. For those who persistently dig their heels into the ground, preparing to resist what they don't want to hear, they'll possibly never have a clear sense of God's purpose for their lives—perhaps one of their own making, but not necessarily the thing God has called them to do. The same is true for those who require that God speak so loudly and so dramatically that they will never again be able to doubt. Those waiting for a dramatic sign or an audible voice from heaven might never hear or see it because, deep down, they are being ruled by a fearful heart or an unsurrendered will.

NO MOVEMENT, NO STEERAGE

Many times, people discover their calling only as they take a step of faith to go. Filipinos have been going into all the world for over a hundred years, not necessarily as Christian missionaries, but as crew members on shipping vessels. Ronnie Pedroso, who goes to Victory, is captain in charge of a bulk cargo ship that is constantly moving all over the world. He shared with me a simple illustration about steerage and movement: "Sitting dead in the water you can stand at the helm and spin the wheel in either direction without effect. It's only when you're under way, when water is moving across the rudder, that you are able to steer the vessel. No movement, no steerage."

Captain Pedroso's illustration immediately reminded me of Demy and Soc Reyes, medical doctors who, from 1989–2001, had operated a small private hospital in Silang, Cavite. They primarily served the local people, including several members and families of pastors from various Victory churches in the Philippines. They were both dedicated disciples and small group leaders. They eventually became pastors in their province, and then in Victory Manila. When an opportunity opened for us to visit and scout out the nation of Cambodia in 1993, I invited Dr. Demy to join me on the trip. His recollection:

> I experienced an overwhelming burden and a sense of discomfort that I could not seem to understand the first time I went to Cambodia with Pastor Jun. We visited one of the most notorious prisons, Security Prison 21, where an estimated 20,000 Khmers were repeatedly tortured and forced to name family members and close friends, who in turn were also arrested, tortured, and eventually killed. That's when my heart broke with compassion for the Khmer people. This burden never left my heart, even after several years. The experience became a dream and a mission that I needed to fulfill.

After the short-term mission trip, Dr. Demy said to me, "Jun, this is all your fault. You've ruined us!" I was relieved to see that he had a big smile on his face as he blamed me for ruining his life. I think what he meant was that the Cambodia trip ruined him and his wife for doing anything else because it confirmed what they had been sensing—the Holy Spirit's calling to relocate to Cambodia as missionary church planters.

And so, in their late fifties, Demy and Soc became rookie missionaries to the great nation of Cambodia, and also became two of the oldest graduates of Every Nation Leadership Institute's School of World Missions. They finally landed in Phnom Penh, Cambodia, in April 2010. Through evangelism and compassion ministries like providing medical services and starting an orphanage, the Every Nation church in Phnom Penh, Cambodia, has made an impact in the lives of many students, some key government officials, and close to 2,000 surviving victims of the Khmer Rouge genocide. The church has planted churches in Battambang and the eastern part of Phnom Penh, and has also produced numerous local leaders who have become pastors, evangelists, campus missionaries, and short-term missionaries overseas.

GLOBAL MISSIONS CHALLENGE

Examining ourselves in the light of the Moravian missions movement is quite appropriate. We look carefully at their example because of their willingness to say, "Here I am. Send me!" Below are a few challenges for those who are contemplating serving as long-term missionaries in Every Nation.

Perseverance and Funding

Building a ministry partnership team and raising the necessary funds often serve as a filter for those who sense a call to mission, either at home or abroad. Some will abandon the mission at the onset when they discover that they'll need to convince others of their calling to assemble a team of financial partners. The example of the first two Moravian missionaries, as well as those who followed, raises the questions: How convinced are you of God's calling? And how persistently will you pursue it? Even if you are called to a paid-staff position in the church, the challenge to trust God for extraordinary funding will eventually find you. You may never become the leader God has called you to be if you are unable or unwilling to stand in faith in the face of significant financial challenges.

Holy Discontentment

God's calling to missions, like His calling to any other pursuit, can come upon us in many ways. For Demy and Soc, the holy intolerance for what was going on in Cambodia became a clear calling for the next stage of their lives. They went, saw that the harvest was plentiful but the laborers few, then said, "Here we are, send us."

Sometimes the still, small voice of the Holy Spirit speaking to us is all it takes to empower us with unshakeable confidence about what we are called to do. Others seem to have been arrested by the Holy Spirit simply by hearing a report about people in need. In August of 1753, Count von Zinzendorf spoke to a congregation of Moravians at Fetter Lane in London. He described how and when he had first caught the desire for missions.

I know the day, the hour, the spot in Hennersdorf . . . I heard items read out of the paper about the East Indies, before regular reports were issued; and there and then the first missionary impulse arose in my soul.

Here's how that holy discontentment affected Nehemiah, one of the Jews of the Babylonian captivity, who rose to become the trusted cupbearer of King Artaxerxes.

> Now it happened in the month of Chislev, in the twentieth year, as I was in Susa the citadel, that Hanani, one of my brothers, came with certain men from Judah. And I asked them concerning the Jews who escaped, who had survived the exile, and concerning Jerusalem. And they said to me, "The remnant there in the province who had survived the exile is in great trouble and shame. The wall of Jerusalem is broken down, and its gates are destroyed by fire." As soon as I heard these words I sat down and wept and mourned for days, and I continued fasting and praying before the God of heaven.
>
> —Nehemiah 1:1–4

Praying about the intolerable situation of Jerusalem and the remnant of the Jews living among the ruins was not enough for Nehemiah. He became a fundraiser, a mobilizer, and an advocate for the rebuilding of the walls of Jerusalem. His confidence and sense of divine calling began as a holy discontentment.

The first Moravian missionaries followed a similar path to God's calling. They heard reports of the conditions among the slaves in the Caribbean Islands that they considered so intolerable that something had to be done. As they prayed, the Holy Spirit put it into their hearts that they were the ones to do it. When Leonard Dober was asked his reasons for going to St. Thomas, he composed a letter describing his motivation:

> When the gracious Count came back from his trip to Denmark and told me about the slaves, it gripped me so that I could not get free of it. I vowed to myself that if one other brother would go with me, I would become a slave, and would tell him so, and [also] what I had experienced from our Savior.

Nehemiah, Zinzendorf, Leonard Dober, and Demy Reyes had similar experiences. Their hearts were gripped by the news of people in foreign lands who were deprived or oppressed. The Holy Spirit seems to have quickened their hearts so that the situations became completely intolerable to them. The reports resulted in a kind of righteous anger, which became a calling for some of the most improbable accomplishments in history—the rebuilding of the walls of Jerusalem, the return of the Jews from captivity in Babylon, and the Modern Missions Movement.

Surrendered Hearts

Perhaps it was the spiritual atmosphere among the Moravians at Herrnhut, that is, the universal atmosphere of surrender among their congregation, that made it easier to hear the calling to go with such clarity. Don't misunderstand me—an unconditionally surrendered heart doesn't mean an automatic calling to go. God is just as likely to call you to stay. The point is, whether you'll go or stay, you'll never have real clarity about God's purpose and plan for you without a surrendered heart. Denying your own will in order to surrender to God's is a daily battle and a lifelong journey of discipleship. But one of the signs that you have correctly discerned His calling is that when the wrestling match is over, you feel a tremendous peace and confidence about what He's calling you to do. It's a sense of greater grace, empowering your faith to accept the challenge to pray, give, and go.

Chapter 7

Student Missionary-Sending Movements

It is our duty to evangelize the world because we owe all men the Gospel.

—Dr. John R. Mott
Chairman of the Executive Committee, Student Volunteer Movement

For if I preach the gospel, that gives me no ground for boasting. For necessity is laid upon me. Woe to me if I do not preach the gospel!

—1 Corinthians 9:16

THE 150-YEAR HISTORY of global missionary-sending movements among college students is simply astounding. Like many other such movements, one movement has led to the next, which has led to the next, and so on. For example, the Moravian missionary-sending movement became one of history's most remarkable movements. John Wesley came to saving faith in 1738 as a result of several encounters with Moravian missionaries. Returning to London from a failed mission venture, John Wesley reluctantly attended a Moravian meeting at Aldersgate at which his heart was "strangely warmed." That same week his brother, Charles, had a dramatic encounter with the Holy Spirit. The Wesleys were among the prime movers of the Evangelical Revival. George Whitefield is generally considered to be the most influential preacher of the Great Awakening that swept across America in the 1740s. Twenty-six years later, William Carey at his first meeting of the Northampton ministers' association challenged the church in its obligation to go into all the world to proclaim the gospel. Later, Carey credited his missionary inspiration—and the birth of what would come to be known as the Modern Missions Movement—to the Moravians.

Instead of thinking about missionary-sending movements as separate and distinct seasons of expansion, each movement is really just a continuation of one grand movement—the Great Commission. These various movements are all connected in one way or another; if not by the actual association and transfer of the vision, then by the sovereign moving of the Holy Spirit calling individuals out of obscurity to go into all the world as missionaries.

There was a Second Great Awakening in America in the first half of the nineteenth century, followed by a Third Great Awakening in the latter part of that century, inspired largely by the preaching of D.L. Moody (1837–1899). The demographic that was most awakened by this third awakening was college students. As long as there have been universities, there's never been an era in which **some** university students were not going **somewhere** to do **something** for Christ. However, it was D.L. Moody's influence that inspired college students through different movements to begin going into all the world by the tens of thousands.

THE CAMBRIDGE SEVEN

D.L. Moody visited Cambridge University in 1883, and this is when the seed of student missions was first planted. Moody actually went to Cambridge with significant reservations. He was a plainspoken revivalist with meager education, invited to speak at the world's foremost center of academic learning. His down-to-earth approach was evident on one occasion in London when an over-eager clergyman was presenting a prayer that seemed to be without end. Moody suggested to the audience, "Let's all just sing a little while the reverend finishes his prayer." That type of audience interaction was greatly entertaining for a crowd of commoners, but equally inappropriate for those who considered themselves part of the high church and high-minded at Cambridge University.

In the beginning, most of the Cambridge students came to mock the crude American evangelist, but after several days the chief antagonist among the students approached Moody and repented. That individual's change of heart transformed the mood of the entire assembly. The preaching of the gospel began to bear fruit among the Cambridge students. The seed grew quickly and multiplied at least a hundredfold, not only in the number of student conversions, but eventually in the passion by which those students engaged in global missions.

Moody spent three years in England. From 1883 to 1885, five current and two former students from Cambridge—who had already received commissions in the British Army—volunteered to serve with Hudson Taylor's China Inland Mission. They had all been former friends and Cambridge athletes—rowers, runners, and cricket players—who through Moody's preaching had made the commitment to follow Christ wherever He might lead them. What was most notable was that these seven Cambridge students who were dedicating their lives to cross-cultural missions were young men from the most distinguished families in British society.

Prior to their departure, the seven toured the campuses of England and Scotland, holding meetings for the students. Everywhere they went, the meeting places were filled. Hundreds were converted each night through their simple but moving testimonies about the grace of God in their lives and why they were going to China. Their witness for Christ even made its way to Queen Victoria, who was pleased to receive a booklet containing the testimonies of the group now known as the Cambridge Seven.

The chairman of the China Inland Mission said at their send-off:

> Together they have given themselves to the work of God in China; not only relinquishing brilliant prospects and social distinction, to become poor missionaries, but actually joining the China Inland Mission, which means so much! They are going to put on Chinese dress and braided tail; going to bury themselves, nobody knows where, in the heart of that strange land, to live in the people's houses and eat their food, and rough it in long, trying journeys and all sorts of other ways.

In February 1885, the seven sailed for China and arrived at Shanghai on March 18, 1885. They were followed in subsequent years by scores of students who, under their influence, had given themselves to Jesus Christ to reach other parts of the world.[1]

THE MOUNT HERMON ONE HUNDRED

Three months after the Cambridge Seven sailed for China, D.L. Moody organized a month-long Mount Hermon Bible Conference near Santa Cruz, California.[2] John R. Mott was a student who attended this conference. He eventually became a leader in what came to be known as the Student Volunteer Movement. Here is his account of what happened.

> There came together here at Mount Hermon in the month of July, 1886, 251 student delegates. We came from eighty-nine different universities and colleges. With nine of my fellow-students I came from one of the eastern universities, Cornell University.
>
> A feature of the daily program was the little company—little, I say, although before the conference was over it included nearly every delegate—which met for an hour every morning to discuss methods of carrying on work among our fellow students in the schools and colleges.
>
> At the beginning of this conference nobody had thought of it as being a missionary conference. Several days had passed before the word missions was even mentioned. If I remember correctly, over two weeks had passed before that great theme was suggested on the platform. But there were causes hidden in the background.
>
> [At Princeton, a missionary's son and daughter, Robert and Grace Wilder, had prayed that the Lord would use Mount Hermon to point many to become missionaries. Robert, a Princeton undergraduate, went to the conference, Grace prayed for it steadily at home. Back at her own college, Mount Holyoke, she was one of thirty-four young women who a few years before had signed a declaration: "We hold ourselves willing and desirous to do the Lord's work wherever He may call us, even if it be in a foreign land."
>
> Meanwhile, July 16th saw the first missionary address in an evening meeting, and another followed within a week.]
>
> Then came a meeting that I suppose did more to influence decisions than anything else, which happened in those memorable days. . . . We went out of that meeting not discussing the speeches. Everybody was quiet. We scattered among the groves . . . I know many men who

prayed on into the late watches of the night. The grove back there on the ridge was the scene that night of battles. Men surrendered themselves to the great plan of Jesus Christ for this whole world.

The conference was drawing to a close when another meeting was held of which we do not talk much. . . . It was held in the old Crossley Hall. We were meeting there in the dusk. Man after man arose and told the reason why he had decided to become a volunteer.

At the beginning of the Mount Hermon Conference fewer than half a dozen students were expecting to be missionaries. By the last day ninety-nine had decided and had signed a paper that read, "We are willing and desirous, God permitting, to become foreign missionaries." Ninety-nine had signed that paper.

The conference closed, but the next morning those ninety-nine met for a farewell meeting of prayer. As I recall, it was in a room in Recitation Hall. While we were kneeling in that closing period of prayer the hundredth man came in and knelt with us.[3]

Robert Wilder spent the following academic year touring American college campuses and telling the story of the Mount Hermon One Hundred. The decision to go was not an easy one. Wilder's father was sick and close to death. After two days of prayer and consideration, Robert's father called him into his study and said, "Son, let the dead bury their dead. Go and preach the kingdom." Starting in Maine, Wilder and his traveling companion visited 162 campuses over the following eight months, and over 2,000 college students pledged themselves to become missionaries.[4]

To preserve the renewed vision for world evangelism, in 1888, the Young Men's Christian Association (YMCA) leaders organized the Student Volunteer Movement (SVM) for international missions. They placed John R. Mott, one of the Mount Hermon One Hundred who had recently graduated from Cornell, at its head. The movement formed organizations on college and seminary campuses across the nation. Students signed pledge cards stating their intention to become missionaries and joined weekly meetings to study missions. The watchword of the movement was "The Evangelization of the World in This Generation." The SVM became one of the most effective missionary-mobilizing movements to date. Before it was formed, the missionaries supported by American Protestants were less than 1,000. But from 1886 to 1920, 8,742 missionaries in the United States joined the organization. Twice that number left the country to do missions work, inspired by the SVM without ever becoming members.[5]

In 1891, 558 students representing 151 educational institutions attended the first SVM Convention in Cleveland, Ohio. Four years later at a second Cleveland convention, there were 6,200 student volunteers from 352 institutions. All of this happened within five years of the Mount Hermon Bible Conference. In 1920, the peak year statistically, 2,783 students signed the SVM decision cards at the convention in Des Moines, Iowa, and in 1921, 637 sailed for the mission field.[6]

BORDEN OF YALE

In his book *100 Years from Now*, Pastor Steve recounts the story of Borden of Yale:

> William Borden could be considered one of the greatest campus missionaries, or one of the greatest Christian givers, or one of the greatest Christian ministers ever. Take your pick. He was an extraordinary example of each.
>
> William was born in 1887 into the significant wealth of a Chicago attorney . . . He became a Christian at an early age and first felt the call to be a missionary while on a round-the-world tour before entering Yale University.
>
> Despite having experienced numerous spiritual awakenings since its founding in 1701, when Borden arrived on the campus in 1905, rationalism and skepticism had permeated Yale from top to bottom.
>
> A group of incoming freshmen led by Borden began a network of prayer meetings that turned into a campus revival. As is often the case, the revival was met by opposition, and the primary opposition was from Yale professors. Nonetheless, by Borden's senior year, one thousand of the thirteen hundred students at Yale were meeting in small discipleship and prayer groups.

Borden and a few friends traveled to Nashville for the 1905 Student Volunteer Movement conference, held every fourth year. Dr. Samuel Zwemer, missionary to Egypt and an expert on Islam, displayed a map that marked every mission station from China to West Africa, showing at the same time the vast areas with no Christian witness. Borden returned to Yale committed to being a missionary among the Muslims in Kansu, a remote region of China considered to be one of the most difficult mission assignments on earth.

After graduating from Yale and then Princeton seminary, Borden spent three months speaking on over thirty campuses. According to the general secretary of the Student Volunteer Movement, the impact of Borden's dedication and testimony "were the most fruitful three months of the movement."

On December 12, 1912, Borden sailed for language school in Egypt. Within the first two weeks in Cairo, he had organized seminary students to distribute the *Khutbas* (a booklet by a converted Muslim) to the entire city of eight hundred thousand people. Within three months of his arrival, the young missionary contracted cerebral meningitis, and on April 15, at the age of twenty-five, William Borden slipped into eternity. His last words were scribbled on a piece of paper found under his pillow:

No reserve; no retreat; no regrets!

There was scarcely a US newspaper that did not publish a lengthy account of his short life. Memorial services were held all over the world, as well as at the Yale Hope Mission and the African Methodist Episcopal Church where Borden taught Sunday school while in seminary.

A biographical sketch of Borden's life for Muslim readers was published in five languages. Thirty-five thousand copies of the Chinese edition made their way into every province of China and even opened doors for mission stations in previously unreached areas. According to Dr. John R. Mott, the story of William Borden at the 1913 Student Volunteer Movement conference was the most powerful appeal for missionary service ever made by the SVM.[7]

WHAT HAPPENED TO THE MOVEMENT?

In the years that followed the 1920 SVM Convention, there was a rapid decline in convention attendance, as well as the commitments to international missions and the overall vision for world evangelism. It seems that every church historian and missiologist over the last five decades has written some kind of postmortem of the SVM, suggesting various reasons for the demise of such an influential organization. With every opinion I've read, the thought comes to mind: *It's easy to offer advice after-the-fact than to lead in the midst of an ongoing movement.* Looking at their meteoric rise and rapid decline after the 1920s, there are a few things we should consider. I'll briefly share some of my own thoughts, not so much as a eulogy, but looking forward to lessons to be learned for our movement.

The missions strategy of the Student Volunteer Movement focused on recruiting and, to some extent, training as many missionaries as they could. The SVM, however, had neither the finances nor the infrastructure to serve as a missionary-sending organization. They simply relied on denominational mission boards and independent mission-sending societies like China Inland Missions. However, there was soon a long waiting list of recent college graduates saying, "Here I am, send me!"—far more than mission boards could handle. The response from the SVM's senior leaders was that a surplus of students willing to go provided mission-sending entities with a better selection of candidates. The SVM did an extraordinary job of inspiring and recruiting students who were willing to go into all the world as missionaries. Though equipping was available through their on-campus classes at SVM chapters across the country, the SVM could not on its own empower a single missionary to go.

The Student Volunteer Movement was a great recruiter for international missions because that's what it counted. I personally have enormous respect for the SVM. What they accomplished for world missions and particularly for student missions was unprecedented. As the Asia Leadership Team director for Every Nation, I'm constantly trying to inspire and recruit people to go. However, I'm reminded by my experience that what you measure and monitor tends to improve, and what you ignore tends to decline. At Victory we understand that the discipleship journey known as the 4Es is designed to equip and empower small group leaders to engage unbelievers with the gospel. Consequently, the numbers that matter most and the ones we watch most closely are the number of baptisms and the number of small group leaders. In other words, our primary focus is on winning the lost and making disciples. Whenever we begin to focus on the number of people simply attending, the effectiveness of our discipleship process and of the church as a whole declines.

The SVM accomplished things that were downright extraordinary in terms of inspiring and recruiting foreign missionaries. However, in our context, it's not just going into all the world that matters, it's also effectively making disciples once we get there. In his book *The Evangelization of the World in This Generation*, Dr. Mott was very clear and passionate about the need to make disciples of all nations. However, making disciples and training leaders was not something the SVM attempted to measure or monitor. They only counted the missionaries who pledged and went.

Though the Student Volunteer Movement was highly effective at recruiting missionaries, they were far less effective at training leaders. While the senior leaders at the SVM were theological conservatives, second- and third-level leaders eventually emerged, many of whom did not share those same beliefs. At the senior level, the SVM lacked the ability or foresight to establish an effective leadership development process. At Victory, we refer to that as leadership multipliers—identification, instruction, impartation, and internship. (For an in-depth look into this, read *The Multiplication Challenge* by Steve Murrell and William Murrell.) Organizational sustainability is not about a succession plan for a single leader, but a leadership development plan for battalions of leaders at all ages and stages to serve at all levels of the organization. In short, the SVM and its second- and third-level leadership evolved in the same manner as the individual missionaries themselves—by recruitment. Winning, discipling, developing, and sending leaders from our own churches is a slower process, but one that creates a far more sustainable movement because it builds upon a common foundation.

The Student Volunteer Movement relied on a single idea as the rallying point. The organization focused primarily—some would say almost exclusively—on the vision of world evangelism. That unifying principle worked well enough at the beginning. The 251 attendees at the Mount Hermon Bible Conference in 1886 came by invitation. They were students known to have an established biblical foundation. The SVM tried unsuccessfully to straddle the ever-widening theological gap between liberal and conservative positions on theology and missiology based on the bigger vision: the evangelization of the world in this generation. However, the issue of biblical and doctrinal faithfulness became more and more critical as time went on. More than anything else, the lack of a solid theological footing was the crack in the foundation that eventually brought the whole house down. The mission objective of the SVM was so lofty and so noble, it was assumed that establishing biblical foundations would take care of itself.

Through five decades, the SVM was directly or indirectly responsible for 20,000 student and postgraduate missionaries who served abroad. However, as they approached the 1930s they seemed to have lost their way, having progressively departed from solid doctrinal and missiological positions in favor of humanistic and social-gospel concepts. What would D.L. Moody have thought? The SVM became more and more irrelevant, having compromised away its power and appeal. It struggled along for another four decades before a rather unceremonious decision to terminate the organization.

Many point to the post-World War I pessimism as a contributor to the SVM's decline. However, the response from students at the 1920 convention in Des Moines was the height of the SVM. I think it was more the abandonment of both an evangelical theology and the burden for the lost that contributed to the radical decline. The students with missionary inclinations simply looked for other organizations that began to emerge.

THE MISSIONARY MOVEMENTS THAT FOLLOWED

The Student Foreign Missions Fellowship (SFMF) was organized in 1938 by student leaders, and chapters were formed throughout the United States and Canada. Seven years later, SFMF merged with the campus ministry InterVarsity Christian Fellowship (IVCF), becoming IVCF's missions department. SFMF aimed to hold regular international conferences on student missions. The first was held in 1946 in Toronto, Canada, and the second was held in 1948 on the Urbana campus of the University of Illinois. This conference, eventually called the Urbana conference, has been held every three years since. Over 15,000 delegates attended the twenty-fourth Urbana Missions Conference in 2015, with 9,416 students making commitments to cross-cultural missions.[8]

In 1884, under the preaching of D.L. Moody, the Cambridge Seven committed their lives to serve as missionaries to China. A hundred years later in 1984, as already mentioned, sixty-five American student missionaries arrived in the Philippines to conduct an outreach among Filipino students in the University Belt of Metro Manila. To date, 419 cross-cultural missionaries from Every Nation are serving around the world. Whether they realize it or not, every college student on a summer mission trip and every recent graduate dedicating his or her life to global missions is following in the footsteps of the Cambridge Seven, the Mount Hermon One Hundred, and the tens of thousands of students inspired to go because of the Student Volunteer Movement.

THE CASE FOR CAMPUS MINISTRY

Between 2000 and 2014, the number of students in higher education institutions around the world more than doubled, rising from 100 million to 207 million. In the same period, the global higher-education enrollment ratio increased from 19 to 34 percent. This ratio expresses enrollment as a percentage of the population who are in the five-year age group immediately following secondary school graduation. In other words, one-third of all young people ages nineteen to twenty-three are college students studying somewhere in the world. By 2025, the number of students around the globe enrolled in higher education classes will have increased to more than 262 million.[9]

Campus ministry has always been central to our mission. In fact, Every Nation never makes a decision to go anywhere in the world without asking: Where are the university students, and how can we reach them? Dr. Rice Broocks's "Campus Manifesto"[10] explains eight reasons we prioritize campus ministry:

1. Major movements, bad or good, start on the campus. Want to see where the world is going? All you need to do is look at college campuses. That's where the future is being formed. The communist revolutions of the mid- to late-twentieth century, the Student Volunteer Movement, the sexual revolution and the radical leftist organizations of the 1960s, the Jesus revolution of the 1970s, the student demonstrations against South African Apartheid at Berkeley and Columbia Universities—they all began on college campuses.

2. The majority of those who become Christians do so as students. C.S. Lewis's Screwtape (the devil's senior advocate) might even say, "If we can get people through college without them becoming Christians, then we've all but got it made. Even if we lose them to Christ later on, at least it will be far less likely that they will become pastors or missionaries."

3. International students impact their nations. There are over 1.2 million international students on U.S. campuses alone, and these international students represent the top 1 percent of their nations' elite. In the Philippines, international students from nations such as India, Japan, Korea, Nepal, and Pakistan study on our campuses. We currently have children of global business leaders, government officials, and royalty in Every Nation Campus. Internationals studying in major countries all over the world often become church planters in their home countries.

4. The values on campus become the values in society. Ethics and philosophy taught by professors on university campuses will over the next decade slowly but surely work their way into public policy, media, and education. As a result, those ideas and values are perpetuated through legislation, public school education, movies, literature, and media.

5. The future leaders of society are in the campuses. Students are comparatively open and impressionable. And even if they do not become Christians, the Christians they meet will influence them. And if there is no Christian witness on the campus, what are students to conclude but that Christ is irrelevant to the values, lifestyle, and philosophies they are learning in college? After they become leaders, it's very difficult to get to them and inspire radical change.

6. The most available and trainable groups of people are on our campuses. Students are at universities in search of what they will do with their lives. Since they don't have a lot of obligations, they are the ones most unhindered when it comes to following Christ and answering the call to serve Him. The campus is not only the source of the next generation of secular leaders, but also Christian leaders and missionaries as well.

7. When we reach a student, we reach a family. A family member becoming a Christian as a student will often influence mothers and fathers, brothers and sisters. If a parent becomes a believer, it often changes the destiny of their children. If we abandon the campus, we abandon the future. If we persist in winning and discipling students for Christ and training them as Christian leaders, we will change the world.

8. God promised to pour out His Spirit on sons and daughters (Acts 2:17). In other words, we should anticipate and hope for an enormous awakening in the younger generations of the world. We have to respond to this abundance by sending missionaries who are equipped and empowered to make disciples on the campuses.

CHURCH-BASED CAMPUS MINISTRY

When Every Nation was formed in 1994, the three founders shared a common vision—to establish church-based campus ministries worldwide. In fact, many (if not most) of our pastors and campus missionaries became Christians and went through their discipleship journey and leadership training as members of what's now known as Every Nation Campus. They've never known a way of planting churches other than planting them as close as possible to a major campus. Most Every Nation leaders assume it to be the normal way of doing things. However, there's nothing normal about pursuing that mission. This uniqueness is evidenced by the following facts:

↗ There are lots of churches around the world and a lot of campus ministries.

↗ There are also a lot of churches that began as campus ministries.

↗ There are denomination associations that have on-campus presence, such as the Baptist Collegiate Ministries, Chi Alpha Campus Ministries (Assemblies of God), Wesley Foundation (United Methodist), and Reformed University Fellowship (Presbyterian).

However, very rarely do you find a local church that began as a campus ministry that has maintained an ongoing and effective impact on the campus. And if you look for a worldwide movement of churches that all exist with a mission to both the community and university campuses, you will find few examples.

Every Nation has pursued this same mission since its founding, having established church-based campus ministries in eighty of the 195 nations of the world. The Every Nation mission statement has evolved over the years but still reflects that original vision: We exist to honor God by establishing Christ-centered, Spirit-empowered, socially responsible churches and campus ministries in every nation.

EMBRACING TENSION

The Every Nation mission requires many sacrifices in many ways from leaders and members at all levels. It is, as they say, "the cost of doing business" as a church-based campus ministry. And each one of those areas of sacrifice becomes a point of tension. I'm not saying it might possibly create tension—it actually does. There is an ever-present tension associated with the mission of establishing church-based campus ministries in every nation. The reason we've been able to sustain and propagate this model for over twenty years is that we've learned to embrace and live with those tensions. Below are a few of the ongoing tensions with which Every Nation leaders have learned to live.

We embrace the tension of being both local and global. As a worldwide church-planting movement, our mission demands that Every Nation leaders sacrifice by repeatedly sending out and financially supporting their best leaders. Every Nation is by no means the most aggressive church-planting movement, but we want to become one of the most methodical. By God's grace and our church-planting process known as ABC3 (Assessment Center, Boot Camp, Coaching, Consulting, and Clusters), we've been blessed with an extraordinarily high success rate of planting church-based campus ministries.

The Benefits: Every Nation churches are doing their part to fulfill the Great Commission. Over time, mature pastors have learned that sending out great leaders creates space for next-generation leaders to step forward to take their place.

We embrace the tension of being a local church and a church-based campus ministry. I've already mentioned the reality of turnover in college student populations. It's a challenge and a sacrifice to focus on a demographic that is such a poor source of funding. In other words, it requires a significant step of faith to plant a church with a primary mission of reaching college students.

The Benefits: Since the discipleship journey involves engaging students with the gospel, establishing them in the faith, equipping them to minister, and empowering them to make disciples, as a result, there's a continual influx of disciples and next-generation leaders coming up in Every Nation.

We embrace the tension of going and gathering. Getting together for Every Nation leadership conferences and other staff gatherings costs time and money. However, these are the sacrifices that maintain a movement. The costs of gathering create an ongoing tension, but it's a tension that we wholeheartedly embrace.

The Benefits: We are better and stronger together than we are alone. Paying the price for building and maintaining relationships among Every Nation leaders provides essential support, encouragement, and the renewal of our common mission. It's what enables us to continue our mission of establishing church-based campus ministries in every nation.

In every large organization, tensions are usually the result of leaders and followers being required to make sacrifices for the larger mission. In some organizations, those tensions are ratcheted up periodically; in others, the sacrifices are constant because they exist at the heart of the mission. The tensions inherent in an international church-based campus ministry are fundamentally embedded in the mission. The degree to which we find ways to eliminate those particular tensions is the same degree to which we are in danger of wandering away from our central mission. However, we've learned over time that embracing those tensions is the key to our ongoing success.

SUSTAINABLE CAMPUS MINISTRIES

A church-based campus ministry is, in theory, simply what the term describes. However, there are difficulties in that mission that only emerge when you actually work toward accomplishing it. Establishing and maintaining a campus ministry has its unique challenges, including the fact that you lose about 30 percent of your members every year. Two or three lean years in a campus ministry and you're starting from scratch.

Yet, while planting and growing a church is also a challenge requiring a pastor's undivided attention, our ongoing mission doesn't stop with one church or campus ministry. It requires us to continue establishing churches with campus ministries. This is the primary thing that makes us unique among missionary-sending and church-planting movements, and it is accomplished only by leaders who remain focused on that mission. If church planters hope to reach college students and create sustainable campus ministries, they need to raise campus missionaries as quickly as possible—leaders who are devoted to fulfilling the Great Commission in the campuses. Below are a few examples of how Every Nation churches have maintained effective campus ministries over many years.

Victory University Belt, Manila

Victory began in the U-Belt in 1984 with 150 Filipino students. Most of us came from poor families across the Philippines. Senior pastors CJ and Mye Nunag commented on the growth of the U-Belt congregation and the exceptionally high percentage of students involved: "The three critical factors that have enabled the student population at Victory U-Belt to continually reproduce itself throughout the last thirty-five years are geographic location, relentless campus outreach, and leadership development."

Geographic Location. Manila's U-Belt has the highest concentration of colleges and universities in the nation, with an estimated population of 450,000 students studying in at least thirty institutions—all within walking distance from each other. Victory U-Belt is located in the very heart of that district. Simply put, it is a church-based campus ministry— you could even refer to it as a campus-ministry-based church. Either way you think about it, their location is one of the reasons they have been so effective at making disciples from one generation of students to another. They are preaching the gospel to and making disciples of the demographic Every Nation wants to reach. Our mission is to plant churches and campus ministries in every nation. It's one thing to claim that mission as your own—quite another to intentionally locate your church at the heart of the student district.

Relentless Campus Outreach. Since the majority of students go back to their provinces and cities after graduation, leadership succession is a high priority at Victory U-Belt. Given the limited timeframe of students studying and residing at institutions in this area, the leadership team recognizes all too well that if they don't respond to these rapid student transitions, they will quickly lose attendance in their youth services, their stream of campus leaders will dry up, and their effective impact on the campuses will cease. Consequently, they intentionally reach out to high school seniors and college freshmen because they will be on the campuses for more years. When freshmen and sophomores are engaged with the gospel, get established in the faith, and are equipped to make disciples, they'll still have several years to raise new leaders before they graduate.

Leadership Development. Equipping and empowering student leaders are essential prerequisites to sustaining student membership throughout the years. The U-Belt team launched the Leadership Lab—a program to train key student leaders and campus volunteers to assist full-time Every Nation Campus staff. To date, we have fourteen campus missionaries serving in the field, and several more in the process of completing their internship, building their partnership teams, and training to enter full-time ministry. We will soon have twenty-three campus missionaries working on the campuses of the U-Belt.

Grace Bible Church Pearlside, Honolulu, Hawaii

Grace Bible Church Pearlside was planted by Pastor Norman Nakanishi in 1994, and today it has five locations and fourteen services each weekend. At the same time, Pearlside established Every Nation Campus at the University of Hawaii and is now active on four other university campuses on the island of Oahu. The campus ministry out of Grace Bible Church Pearlside has grown consistently and has had hundreds of college students in their services over the course of twenty-five years.

Every Nation Campus at Pearlside employs five building blocks for effective discipleship among the several hundred college students.

Small Group Discipleship. Every Nation Campus at Pearlside experimented with other methods and strategies, but nothing has been as successful as small group discipleship. Depending on the spiritual maturity of a particular small group, they use the previous week's sermon and corresponding study guides provided by campus leaders.

Empowered Leaders. Every Nation Campus at Pearlside does not rely heavily on campus missionaries, but empowers a lot of lay leaders. Their discipleship strategy means that they are constantly training students, recent graduates, and young adult church members. At one point they had over sixty small group leaders discipling students, with 500 attending small groups. It took several years for Every Nation Campus to build up its current momentum. Consistency is crucial in engaging students with the gospel, equipping them to minister, and empowering them to lead.

Engaging Friends with the Gospel. Every Nation Campus at Pearlside and the Every Nation church in Oahu encourage students to engage their friends with the gospel. They don't put a heavy emphasis on mass evangelism. Instead, their often-quoted saying is, "Each one reach one each year." If you ask a student who is part of Every Nation Campus, "Who's your one?" they could probably tell you without hesitation who they were praying for, how often they had invited their friends, or how much of the gospel they had communicated with them.

Church-Based Campus Ministry. Students quickly learn about the value of being part of a church-based campus ministry. Training in giving their testimonies, One-Verse Evangelism, or *THEGODTEST* happens at the church. At one point, so many students were coming that they had two services on the Leeward Community College campus. There's a symbiotic relationship between the Every Nation church and Every Nation Campus. Pastor Norman regularly reminds his congregation, "This is not their campus ministry; it's our campus ministry!" And he makes sure that the campus ministry has every resource they need. He is all in.

Pastors Embracing Campus Ministry. One of the most important things that has enabled Every Nation Campus to have such long-running success is the personal commitment and involvement of Pastor Norman. Billy Lile, the regional campus director, says: "Pastor Norman oversees a large congregation and is a very busy man. Yet he has met with me almost every week since my first day on the job. I know a lot of campus missionaries who serve in parachurch organizations and who also feel very much on their own. Pastor Norman has gone the extra mile many times to make the campus staff understand that we are important parts of his team."

Every Nation Church Stellenbosch, Western Cape, South Africa

The Every Nation church in Stellenbosch began engaging the student community at Stellenbosch University in 1997, and within two years they were officially registered as Every Nation Stellenbosch Society. Through the years there have been challenges to maintaining an effective campus ministry—racial tensions, the controversial language change from Afrikaans to English, and a new university policy that restricted religious meetings in public places. Indoor facilities on this campus are almost impossible to reserve, let alone use, on a regular basis. Thankfully, the church has a facility close to the campus for their services.

Despite these challenges, they continued to experience steady growth and sustain an effective student discipleship program. Over twenty years ago, they began with a couple of small discipleship groups. They now have 250 university students officially registered as Every Nation Stellenbosch Society members and 700 attending the campus service.

The Every Nation church in Stellenbosch is currently pastored by Mark and Marion Griffiths.

Pastor Mark comments:

> From the start, our discipleship culture really helped us to reach students, raise leaders, and perpetuated our on-campus presence. The empowering culture at Every Nation Stellenbosch is evidenced by the fact that students are the ones sharing the gospel, making disciples, and leading the campus meetings. One result of our effort to empower next-generation leadership is that we've always had former students who felt called and equipped to step into the role of

full-time campus missionaries. Those seasoned campus leaders have really made a difference for us.

Every Nation Stellenbosch now has eight full-time campus staff and sixteen more serving the churches and campus ministries in the area. They also encourage students to be aware of issues involving the university community. There is a long history of students from Every Nation Stellenbosch taking on influential leadership positions in student government.

GLOBAL MISSIONS CHALLENGE

The Every Nation churches mentioned above in the Philippines, the United States, and South Africa have been at this for a long time. They've become very focused and strategic about sustaining effective discipleship and leadership development programs among university students. It would be unfair to measure a relatively new Every Nation church plant, or a church plant in a creative-access nation, by those same standards. However, if church planters don't embrace the vision of a church-based campus ministry from the very beginning, it is unlikely they'll fall into it years later. They'll be overwhelmed with the concerns of establishing a typical local church in the community. The challenge for Every Nation missionaries and church planters is their commitment to all the aspects of our mission: We exist to honor God by establishing Christ-centered, Spirit-empowered, socially responsible churches and campus ministries in every nation.

Chapter 8

Global South Missionary-Sending Movement

The era of Western Christianity has passed within our lifetimes, and the day of Southern Christianity is dawning. The fact of change itself is undeniable: it has happened, and will continue to happen.

—Philip Jenkins
Author, *The Next Christendom*

"And I have other sheep that are not of this fold. I must bring them also, and they will listen to my voice. So there will be one flock, one shepherd."

—John 10:16

ACCORDING TO THE CENTER FOR THE STUDY OF GLOBAL CHRISTIANITY at Gordon-Conwell Theological Seminary, in 2018 there were 2.5 billion people who professed to be Christians, about one-third of the world's population. What is happening within those numbers is a major shift in the global distribution of Christians around the world, and consequently a major shift in the geographic center of Christianity. "Major shift" is probably putting it far too lightly. While Christianity in the North (Europe and the United States) has been experiencing a steady decline since the 1960s, most of the explosive growth of Christianity is taking place in the global South (Africa, Asia, and Latin America).

The number of Christians in South Korea, for example, is at 29 percent, when in 1900, only 1 percent was Christian.[1] Today, after the U.S., Korea has sent out the highest number of missionaries, with 27,000 missionaries in seventy nations and the largest churches in the world.[2] Other nations that send out a large number of missionaries are increasingly from the global South: Brazil, China, Colombia, India, Mexico, Nigeria, the Philippines, and South Africa.[3]

Consider the growth of the number of Christians by continent since the beginning of the twentieth century.[4]

Christian Population Percentages

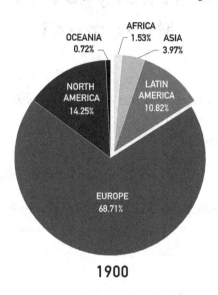

OCEANIA
0.72%

AFRICA
1.53%

ASIA
3.97%

NORTH
AMERICA
14.25%

LATIN
AMERICA
10.82%

EUROPE
68.71%

1900

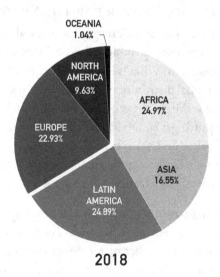

OCEANIA
1.04%

NORTH
AMERICA
9.63%

AFRICA
24.97%

EUROPE
22.93%

ASIA
16.55%

LATIN
AMERICA
24.89%

2018

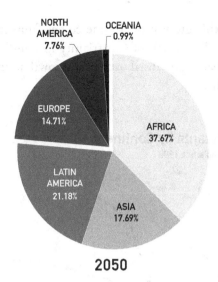

2050

In 1900, Christians in Africa made up 1.53 percent of the total Christian population. Over a hundred years later, they made up 24.97 percent of all Christians, and in 2050 they are projected to be 37.67 percent of the Christian world.

In Asia, Christians were 3.97 percent of the total Christian population in 1900. By 2018, they were 16.55 percent; by 2050, they are projected to be 17.69 percent.

In Latin America, 10.82 percent of the world Christian population was in that region. By 2018, the percentage had increased to 24.89, though by 2050 the number is expected to lower to 21.18 percent.

In 1900, Europe had the lion's share of the global Christian population, at 68.71 percent. By 2018 the number had dropped to 22.93 percent, and in 2050 it is expected to be still lower, at 14.71 percent.

North America had less than 15 percent of the global Christian population in 1900, and it dropped below 10 percent in 2018. In 2050 North America will hold only 7.76 percent of the Christian world.

Lastly, in Oceania in 1900, the small region held only 0.72 percent of the world's Christian population. In 2018 the percentage had increased to 1.04, but in 2050 it is expected to drop again to 0.99 percent.

While part of this growth or decline comes from the birth rates of each continent, the growth of Christianity in non-Christian majority nations shows that a substantial part of the growth in the global South is through evangelism.

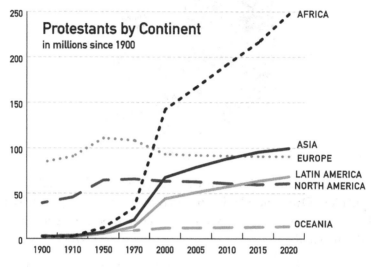

Protestants by Continent.[5] Note: Anglicans are included with Protestants in this analysis.

These numbers come from religious communities, surveys, polls, and censuses that ask for a religious affiliation. Coming from a culture of discipleship, my inclination is to question any worldwide numbers. How many of the 2.5 billion are actively following Christ? How many are nominal Christians? My guess is that the number of genuine followers of Christ tend to be exaggerated in regions where there is a long history of Christianity embedded in the culture. Individuals identify their religious affiliation as Christian because of their heritage, not because of a personal experience with the risen Savior or their commitment as disciples of Jesus. Conversely, numbers are much less likely to be inflated in nations where there's a price to pay for identifying with Christ.

Moreover, if this is true, then the Christian populations in the global North would tend to be exaggerated, and in many nations of the global South would tend to be accurate or underreported—especially in creative-access nations. Consequently, the movements of Christianity to the global South are probably even more dramatic than reported.

It should be noted that the percentage of those identifying as Christians has not increased in the last century. In fact, that percentage has declined from almost 35 percent in 1900 to about 32.6 percent in 2015. Whether you consider those numbers to be inflated or underreported, the statistics show that the rapid decline of Christianity in the global North is being replaced by the rapid increase in the global South.

Not considering examples from the medieval centuries in which kings simply decreed the religion of an entire population, the present growth of Christianity and particularly Protestant affiliations in the global South may well be the largest shift in religious affiliation that has occurred anywhere at any period in history. The geographic center of gravity for Christianity is quickly shifting to regions of the global South. By the year 2050, four out of five Christians will be from the global South, and the Christian world would have shifted firmly to the southern hemisphere. "Within a few decades Kinshasa, Buenos Aires, Addis Ababa, and Manila will replace Rome, Athens, Paris, London, and New York as the focal points of the Church."[6]

We are used to thinking of Christendom as the domain of white Europeans or Americans. However, in the coming decades, the vast majority of Christians will be neither white, American, nor European. According to Pew Forum research, the "average" Christian will be a young Nigerian woman.[7] This southward shift in the modern Christian movement is inevitable simply by population demographics, without factoring in the effect of conversions or departures from the faith. Below are a few of the characteristics of the Christian movement in the global South.

Gospel to the Poor

Because of the population explosions, as well as social, political, and economic realities of the developing world, Christian movements in the global South are dominated by the poor. The contrast to the Christian churches that prevailed in the northern hemisphere for centuries could not be more profound. Christian church members in Europe and America were among the world's most wealthy—the top 1 percent. That doesn't mean every Christian in the global South is living in poverty or that every Christian in the global North is wealthy. However, the overall economic disparity is quite pronounced.

The Gifts of the Spirit

Pentecostal and charismatic expressions of Christianity originated on the day of Pentecost, when the disciples were filled with and empowered by the Holy Spirit. The modern-day revival of the gifts of the Spirit is more evident since the early 1900s. Since then, the number of Christians in the global South identifying themselves as Pentecostal or independent charismatics has grown to over 535 million, or approximately one-third of all Christians in those regions. Membership in these churches is already into the hundreds of millions, and in the near future Pentecostals and charismatics will comprise a much greater percentage of global Christianity—possibly the majority. In southern-hemisphere Pentecostal and charismatic Christian movements, prophecy, healings, exorcisms, dreams, and visions are commonplace. Pentecostal growth is evidenced below.

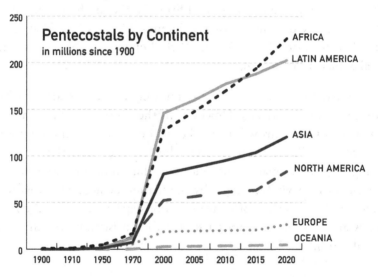

Pentecostals by Continent.[8] Note: Anglicans are included with Protestants in this analysis.

Spiritual Deliverance

For Christian movements in the South, particularly in Africa and parts of Asia, liberation is in part deliverance from supernatural evil. That evil could be seen as the demonic powers of the local witch doctor, but also as corrupt and oppressive authorities being used as instruments of Satan and the powers of darkness.

When Jesus cast out demons and healed people from infirmities, it was a demonstration of His authority over the powers of darkness. Christians in the global South have a much less secularized view of the world than the average Christian in the developed world. The worldview of churches emerging in the southern hemisphere tends to be more biblical and much closer to that of the early church.

Biblical Orthodoxy

Some mainline denominations and seminaries in the global North seem to have become less and less authentically Christian, having questioned or categorically denied fundamental tenets of the faith, such as miracles recorded in the Gospels, the divine inspiration and authority of Scripture, the virgin birth, the Trinity, and the deity of Christ as the Son of God. As it turns out, Christian movements in the global South tend to lean more toward orthodoxy in theology and practice. One example is the conflict within the Anglican Communion—the Church of England and the Episcopal Church in America. An alliance of conservative global South churches flatly accused the Americans and British of departing far from biblical principles: "The unscriptural innovations of North American and some western provinces on issues of human sexuality undermine the basic message of redemption and the power of the Cross to transform lives. These departures are a symptom of a deeper problem, which is the diminution of the authority of Holy Scripture."[9] Since that time, African churches have separated, forming their own Anglican Communion with many conservative Episcopal churches joining them. In the words of Kenyan archbishop Benjamin Nzimbi, "Our understanding of the Bible is different from them. We are two different churches."

Persecution

Both Christianity and Islam are rapidly increasing in the global South as a function of extremely high birth rates in those regions—far higher than the nations in the northern hemisphere. Often, these Christian, Muslim, and some Hindu sects reside together within the same national borders in the global South. As populations rapidly increase, conflicts may become more frequent, enduring, and destructive. From 1950 to 2010, over twelve million Christians died of listed situations of martyrdom. In 1950 to 2000, several of the listed situations were from Eastern Europe and the Soviet bloc. Since 2000, all the listed situations have been in the global South.[10]

Unorganized Beginning

In contrast to the other three missionary-sending movements I've discussed in the previous chapters, there is no single source of the global South movement—no single nation, organization, or church responsible for the growth. There are thousands of missionary-sending churches all throughout the southern regions, such as those in China, India, Nigeria, South Africa, and South Korea. Some are very large churches, while other movements are made up of thousands of congregations in rural villages. Some congregate openly in massive crowds while others meet secretly, leery of spies trying to infiltrate their small groups.

We've heard of stories in different regions of the world like Africa, East Asia, the Middle East, and Latin America where miracles happen frequently, many of them quite astounding. It seems, though, that the leap of faith into supernatural manifestation of healing, divine guidance, and miracles is not so wide. All it requires is faith the size of a mustard seed. Many also point to an atmosphere of corporate faith, while others simply point to the sovereign purposes of God. Whatever the explanation, the movements in the global South seem to be shaped and empowered by the Holy Spirit more than by the strategic plans of one or many missionary organizations.

A Very Different Cultural Context

Phillip Jenkins illustrates the impact of such an expansion into a new cultural context.

> As an analogy, imagine the situation in the seventh or eighth centuries in what was still, numerically and culturally, the Near Eastern heart of Christianity, in Syria or Mesopotamia. Picture a meeting of church leaders who have gathered to hear a report from a traveler from the remote barbarian world of Western Europe. The traveler delights his listeners by telling them of the many new conversions among the strange peoples of England or Germany and the creation of whole new dioceses in the midst of the northern forests. Impatiently, the assembled hierarchs press him to answer the key question: This new

Christianity coming into being, is it the Christianity of Edessa or of Damascus? Where do the new converts stand on the crucial issues of the day: on the Monothelite heresy, on Iconoclasm? When the traveler tells them, regretfully, that these issues really do not register in those parts of the world, where religious life has utterly different concerns and emphases, the Syrians are alarmed. Is this really a new Christianity, they ask, or is it some new syncretistic horror? How can any Christian not be centrally concerned with these issues? And while Syrian Christianity carried on debating these questions to exhaustion, the new churches of Europe entered a great age of spiritual growth and intellectual endeavor.[11]

Reminders of the Early Church

Dreams and visions, healing and exorcisms, miracles of deliverance from persecution, and multitudes coming into the kingdom in ways that are often unpredictable—all these remind me of the early church movement. Like many Holy-Spirit-inspired movements, the early spread of Christianity was unorganized, a bit chaotic, and often controversial in theology and practice. It was, nonetheless, powerful in that it spread based on a common experience with the risen Savior. It changed the world by changing lives one by one.

The pseudo-Christian faith, stripped of all references to the miraculous and transforming power of the Holy Spirit, is quickly dying away. What remain in both the global South and North are Christ-centered, Spirit-empowered, socially responsible movements that are fueling the expanse of the Christian faith. The form and charter of this movement dominated by global South expansions will significantly differ from that of American or European Christianity, and the gap will probably increase in the following decades.

LESSONS FROM THE GLOBAL SOUTH

Every Nation and all other church-planting movements find themselves at a unique time in history. Characteristics of the global South expansion of Christianity are just a few of the realities our missionaries have already and will continue to encounter in the coming era of engaging nonbelievers, making disciples, and planting churches and campus ministries in every nation. Below are some of the applications for Every Nation missionaries and church planters.

1. Continue to focus on next-generation leaders on the university campuses. As a church-based campus ministry, our churches will predominantly be located in urban areas in proximity to university campuses. Our primary mission will be to engage culture and community, make disciples, and train leaders from our congregations. The number of students around the globe enrolled in higher education is forecast to more than double to 262 million by 2025. Nearly all of this growth will be in the developing world, with more than half in China and India alone. The number of students seeking to study abroad could rise to eight million—nearly three times more than today. Though Christianity is rapidly expanding all throughout the global South, spiritual movements on the campuses and among the youth are far less prominent. In Latin America, secularism and agnosticism among university students rival that of the spiritually barren campuses of Europe. But that doesn't mean they don't hunger and thirst for the truth and won't respond to an appropriate explanation of the gospel. Here's one example.

God's Not Dead in Bolivia

For centuries, people in Latin America were simply told what to believe, and in recent times students have left the Christian faith in droves. However, when an evangelist showed up proclaiming evidence for faith in Christ, the response from students, educators, and administrators was extraordinary. In April 2017, Pastor Rice and Pastor Fikri Youssef took the *God's Not Dead* seminar to Bolivia for four days on three major university campuses in Santa Cruz. Hundreds more students wanted to attend than could fit in the auditoriums, so Pastor Rice even conducted a mini-presentation for those who couldn't enter. On the last day, 350 students went back to learn more about being a follower of Jesus Christ. Each received a copy of *The Purple Book* in Spanish, translated *El Libro Morado*, which helps new believers build biblical foundations.

2. Become effective spiritual warriors. I've seen that some pastors, even in our movement, are more aware of spiritual warfare than others. At one point, I may even have joked about ministers who imagined that angelic and demonic forces were responsible for every turn of events. Secularists have so discounted the possibility of Satan and demonic powers that even Christians are hesitant to acknowledge their existence, let alone talk about casting out demons. However, as missionaries are sent into regions of the global South, they will increasingly encounter evil spirits who tenaciously defend their territory and possessions. Populations in the southern hemisphere have very different worldviews, far more similar to the first century than to the twenty-first that is so dominated by skepticism and secular humanism.

3. Demonstrate the power of the Holy Spirit. Paul wrote in defense of his calling as an apostle, ". . . my speech and my message were not in plausible words of wisdom, but in demonstration of the Spirit and of power, so that your faith might not rest in the wisdom of men but in the power of God" (1 Corinthians 2:4,5). Missionaries venturing out into some of the less-Christianized regions of the global South find that apologetics (reasons to believe) is more dependent on demonstrations of the person, power, and presence of Jesus than deductive arguments about the existence of God.

A Prayer in the Name of *Isa al-Masih*

There is a city on the Philippine island of Mindanao that is 99 percent Muslim. Sharia law exists here, but without the stoning, amputations, flagellations, or other punishments typically associated with it, which are unlawful in the Philippines. The distribution of alcoholic products and gambling is forbidden and women must cover their heads, though non-Muslims are exempted from this rule. To date, Mindanao is a region where Al-Qaeda has established a strong presence.

In September 2018, Jonathan, leader of the Peace Project, made a disciple in this city by simply challenging a new believer with a Muslim background to pray for a miracle in the name of Jesus (*Isa al-Masih*). Jonathan went to a university in the city weekly to engage Muslim students in a discipleship group. One student, who happened to be a spy for an Islamic propagator group at the university, was curious as to why one of his closest friends was going every weekend to Jonathan's group. He started connecting with Jonathan online. At first, Jonathan was reluctant to talk to the spy and avoided him. He was afraid of what he had heard and sensed from the other believers in the group. The other students were afraid of him, because of his affiliation and position in the Islamic group. But every time Jonathan prayed, the spy's name and face would pop into his head, until one time, the Lord asked him, "Why are you afraid? I love this person." Obeying and trusting the Lord, Jonathan contacted the spy and invited him to their discipleship group. The spy heard the gospel on the day he joined the group and became a believer. Jonathan began establishing him in the faith using a discipleship tool specifically created for Muslims to understand their newfound faith in Jesus.

Another time in their discipleship group, they were talking about the power of the name of Jesus. While they were talking, the Holy Spirit encouraged Jonathan to invite the others to ask Him for something impossible using the name of Jesus. The spy left the meeting, but couldn't stop thinking about Jonathan's invitation and the Scripture they had read (Revelation 19:11–16). That night in bed, he prayed in the name of Jesus about something that seemed impossible: the approval of his proposal to propagate Islamic teachings in a certain school. So much time had passed since the proposal that he was certain it had been denied or forgotten.

That night, he had a vivid dream of the scene from Revelation 19:11–16— Jesus was riding on a white horse, clothed in a robe dipped in blood. In his dream, he saw himself clothed in a white robe following Jesus. The next morning he was awakened by a phone call from the assistant principal of the school, telling him that his proposal had been approved. Amazed and overwhelmed, he went to talk to Jonathan about his encounter with Jesus and asked Jonathan to help him know more about his newfound faith. Within a month of hearing the gospel, the former spy was baptized in water.

Jonathan told him about the Great Commission and his vision of blessing and reaching Muslims for Christ, and that he felt like he was the only one proclaiming the gospel to the lost people in Mindanao. To this, the former spy replied: "Big brother, now we are two."

Jonathan is grateful that by the grace of God, he obeyed and responded in love, not fear. He learned that the only way we can reach Muslims in our nation is by fully trusting God and extending His love to them.

Stepping out in faith confidently and trusting God to show up in your behalf is a significant challenge for any missionary, but a particularly high hurdle for those unfamiliar with the presence and power of the Holy

Spirit. This is also true for those who believe in the Holy Spirit but have not yet experienced His power.

4. All things are possible with God—anywhere in the world. The Pew Research Center published a report from their Religious Landscape Survey in 2015. The clear trend was that those who may have previously identified themselves as nominal Christians were changing their religious affiliation to "none."[12] Dr. Ed Stetzer, Billy Graham Distinguished Chair of Church, Mission, and Evangelism at Wheaton College, responded with three takeaways of his own. First of all, "convictional Christianity" is rather steady. The falling away has been primarily those previously identifying themselves as "nominal Christians." Secondly, there has been a significant shift within American Christianity. In the 2014 survey, 50 percent of all Christians identified themselves as "evangelical" or "born again" (a 6 percent increase from the 44 percent in 2007). Thirdly, mainline Protestantism continues to hemorrhage. Only 45 percent of those raised in the mainline Protestant tradition remain in those churches. There seems to be a flight among Christians to the more conservative evangelical Protestant churches. The Pew Religious Landscape Survey notes, "The evangelical Protestant tradition is the only major Christian group in the survey that has gained more members than it has lost through religious switching."[13]

And so, by Dr. Stetzer's estimation, the bad news is not so bad after all. But Christianity is no longer as influential in some parts of the U.S. as it used to be, and perhaps biblical awareness has declined, even to its most basic level. Though it's still cool to be a Christian in the rural and southern regions of America, in the densely populated West Coast and Northeast, Christianity is waning—especially among college students.

Nonetheless, Every Nation church planters have made a remarkable impact even in those most gospel-resistant areas. Adam Mabry returned to the U.S. after serving as a missionary in Scotland to plant Aletheia Church in Cambridge, Massachusetts. He did this with his friend Donny Fisher, a campus missionary from Florida. In January 2011, they launched the church a mere half-mile from both Harvard University and the Massachusetts Institute of Technology. Since then, Aletheia Church has grown dynamically. They have planted two other congregations and are currently preparing for a third. About a thousand attend each weekend—

many of them are new believers and a large percentage are students or alumni from the most prestigious universities in North America.

In 2007, Benton County had the distinction of being the most unchurched county in the U.S. Oregon State University (OSU) in Corvallis is located there, and Pastor Seth Trimmer of Grace City Church tells us what Every Nation Campus is doing in his alma mater.

> Since 2007, we have grown so that 300 to 400 students are a part of our church. We've raised four full-time campus missionaries with more to come in the next year. Dozens of interns and student leaders have engaged students on the campus, doing *THEGODTEST* hundreds of times and presenting the gospel to students who have never heard it before.

Since OSU is primarily a college town, most of the post-graduate job opportunities are found in Portland. In the last few years, Grace City Church in Corvallis has planted churches in Eugene near the University of Oregon, and in Portland near Portland State University. When disciples graduate from OSU, they are connected with Every Nation churches in the region. Today, Benton County is no longer the most unchurched county in the United States, due in part to Grace City's impact on the campus and community.[14]

History has shown that while there have been periods of great decline in churches in the U.S., seasons of extraordinary revivals have swept across the entire nation. Now, though, Americans who profess to be Christians in some areas of the country have to live out their faith as part of a minority. Though they may have never experienced real persecution, they are becoming more and more a disenfranchised group. Yet, as we know, Christianity has always been at its best when it goes against the status quo.

GLOBAL MISSIONS CHALLENGE

The global missions challenge for all Every Nation pastors, missionaries, and church planters is to embrace cultural realities as opportunities to make disciples **of all nations** (the Greek phrase, *panta ta ethne*, means "of all ethnicities"). Five times in the book of Revelation, this phrase is used: "people from every tribe and tongue." Several times the word "nation" is included. Christ has purchased by His blood people from every nationality, ethnicity, and language. Though our mission statement clearly specifies that we establish Christ-centered, Spirit-empowered, socially responsible churches and campus ministries, we also work to ensure ethnic diversity. Establishing all white, all black, all brown, or any other ethnically exclusive expression of Christianity is not consistent with our mission. That's not to say that leading a church that is inclusive of Christian disciples from different ethnicities is easy. But ethnically diverse churches and campus ministries are an answer to prayer—Jesus' prayer that God's kingdom would come and His will would be done on earth as it is in heaven.

Moreover, Christianity is alive and growing exponentially. Not only is the majority of southern-hemisphere church planting the result of initiatives in the global South, we are planting churches in Europe and North America as well. We send missionaries to the places the Holy Spirit has called them to, in response to what Jesus said: "The harvest is plentiful, but the laborers are few. Therefore pray earnestly to the Lord of the harvest to send out laborers into his harvest" (Luke 10:2). We don't presume to be able to change God's purpose or direction for a particular missionary, yet we are instructed to earnestly pray for laborers to go into the places where the harvest is plentiful. We have a lot to be thankful for and many successes to celebrate. However, we've barely scratched the surface of our stated mission. We need hundreds of missionaries who are called by the Holy Spirit, equipped, and empowered to go into all the world, both the global South and the global North. We need to keep on doing the same old boring strokes of discipleship, but at the same time pray in earnest that God would call more laborers from our midst and send them out into His harvest.

3 FULFILLING THE EVERY NATION MISSION

Trust the past to God's mercy,
the present to God's love and
the future to God's providence.
— *Saint Augustine*

Unless the Lord builds the house,
those who build it labor in vain.
Unless the Lord watches over the city,
the watchman stays awake in vain.
— *Psalm 127:1*

PART
THREE

2005

I THINK OF EVERY NATION as being caught up in the waters of a fast-flowing stream. We can see the river banks quickly passing by, but without that fixed point of reference, our only sense of movement is the result of our efforts to paddle. In reality, however, our progress is primarily the result of being caught up and carried along in the movement of the Holy Spirit. Periodically, we need to step back and consider how much the sovereignty of God and the power of the Holy Spirit have been the reason for our progress thus far.

Historical perspective is good for us. We should remember that the outpouring of the Spirit and the infusion of His gracious ability are not automatic—good reasons for humility and prayer. There have been seasons in which progress in world evangelism and Christian discipleship were easily attained because missionary-sending movements were simply paddling with a very strong current. There have also been seasons in history in which the waters were stagnant, and even the slightest progress was attained with enormous effort and sacrifice. And then there are those seasons in which the tides have flowed very strongly against the church. I'm reminded of how we view going to creative-access nations: Green means "go," yellow means "go faster," and red means "go anyway."

I think when we look back from eternity, we will discover that most of what we seem to have accomplished was the moving of the Holy Spirit in a special season. We were simply privileged to be caught up and carried along with it. To illustrate that idea, it's like a surfer trying to catch a big wave. The two most important things to do are to get the board pointed in the right direction and start paddling. The power is in the wave, not in the paddling. And the real trick is being able to ride out a big wave without losing your balance and falling off. This last section of the book is my final effort to get us to ride the big wave together in fulfilling the Great Commission by praying, giving, and going.

Chapter 9

Pray with Expectation

The history of missions is the history of answered prayer.

—Samuel Zwemer
Apostle to the Muslims

"And now, Lord, look upon their threats and grant to your servants to continue to speak your word with all boldness, while you stretch out your hand to heal, and signs and wonders are performed through the name of your holy servant Jesus." And when they had prayed, the place in which they were gathered together was shaken, and they were all filled with the Holy Spirit and continued to speak the word of God with boldness.

—Acts 4:29–31

WE ALWAYS EXPLAIN in Every Nation Leadership Institute's School of World Missions that prayer is an essential element of our strategy to reach the nations. That is to say, at the most critical point in our missionary endeavors, there is no organizational strategy (no matter how well conceived) that will give us the direction, boldness, wisdom, provision, or protection that we will need at that moment. That help in times of desperate need will come only from the Helper. It is for that reason we bathe every aspect of our mission in prayer. It is our superstructure—the framework and support of what we go into all the world to accomplish.

Rather than simply reciting a long list of exhortations to pray with expectation, I would like to focus on one critical moment in the history of Christianity, followed by stories from Every Nation. These stories, from both the first and the twenty-first centuries, serve as illustrations of why we must be committed to prayer.

STORIES FROM THE START

In the early days of the first church in Jerusalem, the original apostles, the eleven plus the addition of Matthias who was chosen to replace Judas (Acts 1:12–26), preached this gospel with a fiery boldness that was unprecedented—what might even be considered suicidal. Two dramatic encounters demonstrate the importance of prayer for favor in the wake of bold actions that almost ended the Christian movement abruptly.

Acts 3 and 4 chronicle the healing of the lame beggar, Peter's impromptu message, and the subsequent arrest of Peter and John. The high priest and the Sadducees were filled with jealousy and resentment over what was taking place in the Temple. The ever-increasing popularity of Jesus, along with some astonishing miracles, seemed to confirm the eyewitness testimonies of His closest disciples—that after three days in the grave, Jesus had risen.

The Sadducees were members of a sect that did not believe in any resurrection, let alone the miraculous resurrection of one they considered to be a blasphemer. What especially angered them was not just **what** the apostles were asserting, it was **where** they were doing it. While the synagogue was the home turf of the Pharisees, the Temple in Jerusalem was the source of the Sadducees' power, authority, and privilege. And that happened to be the place of God's choosing for the demonstration of the power and boldness that come from the Holy Spirit.

The Sadducees had the temple guards arrest Peter and John and, on the following day, escorted them from the jail cell to stand before Caiaphas, Annas, and members of the Sanhedrin—the ones primarily responsible for delivering Jesus over to Pilate (Acts 4:5,6). The man who had been lame from birth was also there, standing with the two apostles during this first interrogation. Perhaps he had been arrested for getting healed.

This group of religious leaders had had several confrontations with Jesus over the course of His three-year ministry, none of which turned out very well for them. This, however, was their first official encounter with some of His disciples. The assumption seemed to be that His disciples, primarily a group of rural Galilean fishermen, would not be so bold or courageous in the face of threats and intimidations from the high and holy Sadducees. After all, when the temple guards under the direction of those same religious leaders came by night to arrest Jesus, all His followers had deserted Him. The religious leaders were, however, astonished at the newfound boldness among this same group of Jesus-followers.

The Sadducees ordered them to cease and desist their public proclamation that Jesus had risen from the dead. To this, Peter and John answered: "Whether it is right in the sight of God to listen to you rather than to God, you must judge, for we cannot but speak of what we have seen and heard" (Acts 4:19,20). The two apostles were flogged for their insolence, further threatened, and released.

The Second Arrest

With joyful hearts and bleeding backs, they returned to the others and reported what had happened. The summary of the prayer meeting that followed concluded with these words:

> "And now, Lord, look upon their threats and grant to your servants to continue to speak your word with all boldness, while you stretch out your hand to heal, and signs and wonders are performed through the name of your holy servant Jesus." And when they had prayed, the place in which they were gathered together was shaken, and they were all filled with the Holy Spirit and continued to speak the word of God with boldness.

> —Acts 4:29–31

Obviously, the apostles did not heed the Sadducees' threats and warnings. They went right back to their open-air preaching among the growing multitude of believers continuing to gather in Solomon's Portico. The Sadducees' position in Jewish culture that had accumulated over the previous four centuries was quickly unraveling before their eyes. Something had to be done to stop it. And so, they ordered the temple guards to arrest the troublemakers again. This time all the apostles were thrown into a public prison. "But during the night an angel of the Lord opened the prison doors and brought them out, and said, 'Go and stand in the temple and speak to the people all the words of this Life'" (Acts 5:19,20).

Inexplicably, all the apostles appeared in the Temple the next morning. Instead of trembling in the presence of those who had the authority to have them permanently imprisoned or even executed, this was the response from the apostles:

> "We must obey God rather than men. The God of our fathers raised Jesus, **whom you killed by hanging him on a tree**. God exalted him at his right hand as Leader and Savior, to give repentance to Israel and forgiveness of sins. And we are witnesses to these things, and so is the Holy Spirit, whom God has given to those who obey him."
>
> —Acts 5:29–32

Prior to their first arrest, Peter and John had blamed the crucifixion of Jesus on the general population—as people who "acted in ignorance" (Acts 3:17–26). Now, as all the apostles were standing before the council of religious leaders, their courage and boldness went a step further. They laid the blame for the crucifixion of Jesus right at the feet of those by whom they were being examined (Acts 3:12–26). When the Sadducees and other religious leaders heard this, they went into a rage and wanted to kill all the apostles, just as they had killed their Master (Acts 5:33).

For those who like to entertain counterfactual history (ideas of how the world would be different if only one critical event changed), this was as pivotal a point in history as one could imagine. It's uncertain whether the Sadducees intended to kill the apostles on the spot or bring charges against them that would have led to the same result. Either way, it seemed as if the key witnesses to the Resurrection, the apostolic leaders, and even the future of the Christian faith were all hanging in the balance. Had it not been for one instance of divinely inspired favor, the story of Jesus of Nazareth could have been an obscure footnote in the history of the Jews.

As the council was descending into a murderous mob, Gamaliel, a religious leader and highly esteemed Pharisee, intervened. You might say he stood in the gap or interceded on behalf of the apostles with these words:

> "Men of Israel, take care what you are about to do with these men. . . . keep away from these men and let them alone, for if this plan or this undertaking is of man, it will fail; but if it is of God, you will not be able to overthrow them. You might even be found opposing God!"
>
> —Acts 5:35,38,39

The imprisonment or execution of the apostles was obviously not God's plan. Consequently, He inspired a highly esteemed official who was not necessarily a believer and empowered him with enough courage to jump in front of a runaway train. In standing alone against the rage of the high priest and Sadducees, Gamaliel took a great risk. Whatever clout or favors he had accumulated over the years, this official sensed that it was time to call them all in.

EVERY NATION MISSIONAL TAKEAWAYS

This story says a lot about the power and importance of prayer. Since this was such a seminal event in the survival of the gospel and the first-century church, we should pause for a moment to think about what it means to us—those who, in the twenty-first century, are going into all the world to further spread the gospel and plant more churches. If your motivation is to recapture the approach of the New Testament church, there's no better place to start. And so, here are seven takeaways on prayer from this story and some modern-day examples from our movement.

1. Prayer and Uncommon Boldness. Assuming that timidity is always the safest route is a mistake. We think we should be careful to not offend, not rock the boat, and above all, not speak truth to power. In certain circumstances, however, boldness and prayer inspired by the Holy Spirit become the very means of deliverance.

There are many stories of the Holy Spirit working through Every Nation leaders worldwide, and some are so remarkable that my heart simply burns with excitement. Luke serves as an Every Nation leader in one of the most radical and repressive anti-Christian nations in Asia—also one of the poorest. There are fewer Christians there than in any nation on the planet. Two years ago, Luke was sentenced to many years in prison for preaching the gospel. Many times during the first year he was called to appear before the judge who had sentenced him—representing himself, since no lawyer in that country would dare to identify with a Christian. Luke quoted passages from Acts 23 to 26, and told the judge, "Your most distinguished honor, my conscience is clear before my God and you. I beg you to listen to me patiently as I make my submission in your gracious presence. I have been a Christian for the last twenty-four years of my own free will. No one coerced me to convert to Christianity. To further aggravate you, your distinguished honor, I am now a pastor, and this position will not change no matter what may happen in my life. With all due respect, your honor, it doesn't matter what you do. I will preach the gospel in prison or in the city. It's your choice. But I ask you to give me justice. At this moment, I submit this rebuttal in your gracious presence, your honor."

Proverbs 21:1 says, "The king's heart is a stream of water in the hand of the Lord; he turns it wherever he will." This context also applies to judges and prosecutors. Luke appeared before the court nineteen times in one year and defended his faith in Jesus. With every subsequent appearance before the judge, his sentence was reduced until he was released shortly after the two-year mark. As he was coming out of the court on the final day, the judge greeted him respectfully and told him not to go from city to city to preach the gospel, but to do it in one place as he wished. Simultaneously, the prosecutor exclaimed, "I have served as a government prosecutor for many years. Throughout my career, I have never seen boldness such as you have shown the court. Where do you get this boldness? The God of heaven has seen your heart and released you today from a prison term. I implore you to not take whatever happened in court personally. I was standing there to do my duty as a prosecutor. I wish you all the best for your future." The prosecutor parted with Luke after having given him utmost respect.

Because of his bold faith, Luke was able to have a long conversation with both officials about the gospel.

Here's the most exciting part. The powers-that-be decided to sell off some state property. If a church owns property in that nation, it can designate the facility as a church and hold as many services as it wants. This small, impoverished body of believers in an extremely poor nation raised a third of the funds for the purchase. Every Nation Asia supplied one-third and the final one-third came from American partners. The property is even located less than two kilometers from the nation's only accredited academic institution.

2. Prayer and Boldness from Being Filled with the Holy Spirit. There is no "gift of boldness." I've occasionally heard mission-oriented people pray for courage in the face of opposition, danger, or threats of persecution. I probably shouldn't split hairs over the definitions of boldness and courage, but there is a difference—at least in the application.

Courage is the ability to either endure or attack. When you ask for boldness, it's usually in the context of advancing the cause rather than simply defending or saving it. The apostles were definitely advancing the good news of Christ's resurrection. There was no "bunker mentality" evident with them, even when the whole future of the church and the gospel were at stake. However, they never specifically asked for the gift of boldness or courage. They became bold and courageous as a result of being filled with the Holy Spirit. Twice in this story, Luke (the author of Acts) refers to the apostles being filled with the Holy Spirit just before an extraordinarily bold step of faith.

"Then Peter, filled with the Holy Spirit, said to them . . ." (Acts 4:8). The literal translation of the Greek tense is given in the NASB: Peter spoke with great boldness "having just been filled" with the Holy Spirit.

The second reference is in the church's corporate prayer: "And when they had prayed, the place in which they were gathered together was shaken, and they were all filled with the Holy Spirit and continued to speak the word of God with boldness" (Acts 4:31).

Later on, when Paul and Barnabas were opposed by the sorcerer, Elymas, Luke records the confrontation with the words, "Paul, filled with the Holy Spirit . . . said, 'You who are full of all deceit and fraud, you son of the devil, you enemy of all righteousness, will you not cease to make crooked the straight ways of the Lord? Now, behold, the hand of the Lord is upon you, and you will be blind and not see the sun for a time'" (Acts 13:9–11, NASB).

God doesn't just give us a gift of boldness, He repeatedly fills His servants with the Holy Spirit, and **that** is the source of our boldness. In *100 Years from Now*, Pastor Steve comments on boldness and being filled with the Holy Spirit:

> When asked if they are filled with the Spirit, [Christians] might respond, "Absolutely, I was filled with the Holy Spirit at a Victory Weekend in 2001!" Being filled with the Holy Spirit is not a merit badge to obtain, sew on your shirt, and wear for the rest of your life. Although in Scripture, the baptism of the Holy Spirit is typically a post-salvation experience, the apostles seemed to also consider being filled with the Spirit as a recurring experience. The accounts in Acts

show that they were filled with the Holy Spirit *again*, and they went out speaking boldly *again*.[1]

For thousands of years, Christians have devoted themselves to prayer in order to be certain about their calling and election (2 Peter 1:10). We are forever searching our hearts to discern the leading of the Holy Spirit. But that doesn't end when one finally decides to become a missionary. There's nothing final about that decision. The filling and refilling of the Holy Spirit is a continual pursuit of our devotional lives; it is an ongoing prayer focus.

3. Prayer and the Providence of God. Deliverance is not guaranteed. Perhaps something should be said about boldness that comes from the Holy Spirit in contrast with boldness manufactured by the human soul. Boldness can offend a lot of people and get you arrested, tortured, or even killed. Finding yourself in these extraordinary situations, it's rarely easy to distinguish one from the other, even when looking at the outcome. If missionaries are delivered despite their boldness, some would say that this boldness was definitely inspired and directed by the Holy Spirit; however, if they were not delivered, this proves that their boldness was due to their lack of wisdom. But it's never that simple. Nonetheless, I am confident of this one thing: If God puts you in such a situation and directs you to take an extraordinarily bold stand for your faith, you will experience His grace and the Holy Spirit will empower you in that situation.

The threats, arrests, and crisis prayer meetings continued throughout the early days of the church in Jerusalem, some ending with miraculous deliverance and some not.

> About **that time** Herod the king laid violent hands on some who belonged to the church. He killed James the brother of John with the sword, and when he saw that it pleased the Jews, he proceeded to arrest Peter also. . . . but earnest prayer for him was made to God by the church.
>
> —Acts 12:1–3,5

"That time" referred to the scattering of believers and the persecution by Saul of Tarsus that arose in the wake of Stephen's martyrdom (Acts 11:19,20). James the Apostle, one of the three in Jesus' inner circle (which included Peter and John), was martyred by Herod, and Peter was to be next. The church's earnest prayer for Peter resulted in one of the most notable stories of deliverance in the New Testament. The angel of the Lord removed the chains and unlocked the gates. The servant girl couldn't believe that Peter had been miraculously released. Herod couldn't believe it either and had all the sentries executed (Acts 12:7–19).

You see the conundrum believers in the early church might have faced.

The apostles were miraculously delivered when Gamaliel interceded on their behalf.

Stephen was not.

Saul of Tarsus was saved, but what about those he had thrown into prison?

Peter was even "more miraculously" rescued by angelic intervention.

James was not.

Even James the Just, the brother of Jesus who became the Bishop of Jerusalem, suffered martyrdom. Eventually, that was the fate of most of the apostles.

While twenty-first century Christians in more religiously tolerant regions of the world may have problems understanding why some are delivered and some not, that did not seem to be an issue for first-century believers. The words of Jesus, probably repeated often among the apostles, prepared them and their expectations.

> "You will be delivered up even by parents and brothers and relatives and friends, and some of you they will put to death. You will be hated by all for my name's sake. But not a hair of your head will perish. By your endurance you will gain your lives."
>
> —Luke 21:16–19

4. Prayer and Perseverance. Keep on asking and be in faith to receive. In Luke 11, Jesus told a story to illustrate the power of persistent prayer. A man showed up at a friend's house after a long trip. He arrived unexpectedly around midnight, and there was nothing to eat in the house. So the homeowner went to his other friend's house and knocked on his door to ask for some food. The man inside wouldn't get up to answer because he was not that close of a friend. But the man in need just kept banging on the door. Jesus commented, "I tell you, though he will not get up and give him anything because he is his friend, yet because of his impudence he will rise and give him whatever he needs" (Luke 11:8).

Dihan and Julie Lee were sent out from Grace Covenant Church in Washington, D.C., in Northern Virginia to plant Renew Church L.A. The church was located in between three campuses: University of Southern California, University of California Los Angeles, and Loyola Marymount University. They quickly outgrew their building, and Dihan had his eye on a facility a mile away at West Los Angeles College that would work better for them. They approached the administration about renting a meeting room, but the reply they got was, "No. We've never rented to a church and don't intend to."

Dihan and his leadership team went back to praying and searching for other options. However, they still felt West Los Angeles College was where God wanted them to be. So Dihan went back to ask, but the school was not very responsive. They had to fulfill many requirements to receive provisional permission.

The team kept praying and refused to give up. It took them about eight months of persistent asking to get through the door.

What they finally got was permission to use the facility for one month. It was a trial, with no promises after that.

No church consultant would recommend moving Sunday services to a different location for one month, but they felt led by the Holy Spirit, and so they followed. Afterward, the college official said, "Well, maybe we can do this." They are currently working on a long-term lease. The school granted permits that allowed Renew Church L.A. to use the facility for several months. The church has garnered favor with the local sheriff and campus staff. They even met with the president of the school and are actively partnering with the campus to serve at-risk students.

No amount of training in church planting can take the place of prayer, persistent faith, and being led by God's Spirit. Jesus concludes the story by saying, "Ask, and it will be given to you; seek, and you will find; knock, and it will be opened to you. For everyone who asks receives, and the one who seeks finds, and to the one who knocks it will be opened"

(Luke 11:9,10). Most commentaries note that a literal translation would read, "Keep on asking . . . keep on seeking."

5. Prayer and Extraordinary Wisdom. Words of extraordinary wisdom will come from the Holy Spirit. Many people in our churches around the world prayed earnestly as they followed reports regarding the imprisonment and trial of Mark, who served as an Every Nation pastor in Iran in 2008. Without having very much knowledge about church planting or evangelizing, he had begun the church in Iran by simply praying for his relatives, friends, and anyone who was in need. Those simple actions birthed miracles. Over the next seven years, many were added to their number—more than 300 Iranians received Christ and over 200 were baptized. Of those years, Mark recalled:

> There were so many miracles and so many signs and wonders—things which we saw with our own eyes. If I were to tell them one by one, it would be a very thick book. Cancerous tumors shrinking, evil spirits departing, God speaking to many people in dreams and visions. With house churches now in five other cities, I traveled around Iran every week, encouraging and training new groups of believers. It was just like the book of Acts.

In May 2008, while Mark was meeting with disciples in a park, the Iranian secret police (known officially as the Ministry of Information) raided their meeting and arrested Mark, along with some of the other disciples. Some were questioned and later released, but Mark was kept in solitary confinement. They continually insisted that he repent, deny his faith in Jesus, and go back to Islam. Mark respectfully declined and used the interrogation as an opportunity to preach the gospel to them.

During the third hearing, the judge got tired of Mark's stubbornness and charged him with apostasy. This meant that having lost his faith in Islam, he was considered to be an idolater. If found guilty, he would be hanged.

While in prison, Mark worshiped, prayed, and fasted. He deeply believed that his fellow Christians were earnestly praying for him and that the same miracle that had happened in the book of Acts could happen to him—that somehow God would release him from the hand of the enemy.

Jesus' warnings about being hated, delivered up to authorities, and put to death were immediately preceded by the promise: "This will be your opportunity to bear witness. Settle it therefore in your minds not to meditate beforehand how to answer, for I will give you a mouth and wisdom, which none of your adversaries will be able to withstand or contradict" (Luke 21:13–15).

After four and a half months of solitary confinement and repeated interrogation, Mark found himself standing in the highest criminal court of the Islamic Republic of Iran.

In that final hearing, the judge asked him three questions:

"Is your father a Muslim?"

"Yes, he was," Mark answered, "but he died a long time ago."

"Do you have the fear of God?"

"I do," he replied, "and I'm praying that God will increase it in me."

"Do you want to submit yourself to the hand of God?"

"It is my prayer to know His will and to follow Him."

While the judge was clearly referring to a central tenet of Islam—submission to God—Mark was referring to a decision he had made nine years earlier, one that had and would continue to change his life forever.

The miracle came in the form of an unexpected verdict. After Mark had answered the questions, the judge declared, "Even though you say you are a Christian, I believe that in your heart you are still a Muslim. You are released."

Immediately, an officer of the secret police stood up in the courtroom and pointed to the judge, shouting, "You cannot do this! You are not allowed to release him. You are supposed to execute him. You must make an example of him!" The judge had made his decision, however, and Mark was free to go.

Compass Direct News ranked Mark's story as number six in their "Top 10 Persecution Stories of 2008."[2] Further details of the story have been withheld because many more arrests and interrogations have given away much of the nature, extent, and leadership of the church in Iran to the Iranian secret police.

6. Prayer and Steadfastness. As believers, we are to remain alert and pray continually. In May 2015, 120 Chinese students were attending the annual camp of Every Nation Campus in one of the major cities in China. There was a break on the afternoon of the second day before the closing session. Students were on the beach chatting, sharing life, and playing games. Around 5:30 p.m. they saw a van and a police car speed into the hotel compound. Policemen came pouring out of the van. Immediately, they rounded up everyone on the beach and corralled them into the hotel. They were incredibly swift, and all this happened in just a few minutes. The police began collecting the computers, every piece of printed material, and the names of everyone present.

As soon as our national leaders realized that it was a raid, they instructed the non-Chinese members of our Every Nation team to leave the area. Those three, Jacob and two other Malaysians, began walking away from the hotel. The police officers were shouting at everybody and detaining anyone trying to escape, including six other tourists only a few steps away from the three.

The miracle was that while they were walking away, somehow, the police did not see them. In Jacob's mind, he kept asking, *How could the police not see us when they saw six other tourists right in front of us?* It was as if the Lord had placed an invisible covering over them so that they were able to walk right past the police without being noticed. They kept walking without looking back—down the stairway, away from the hotel, toward the beach. They hid behind a big rock along the shore about 300 meters away from the hotel until almost midnight, interceding for the rest of the church members that were being interrogated.

There's another side to this story. Phuah Boon Leong, a teacher by profession, is a faithful member of our Every Nation church in Kuala Lumpur. Phuah and his wife are intercessors and lead the prayer ministry of the church. While the Every Nation Campus retreat was ongoing in China, Phuah, who was in Kuala Lumpur, had a vision that led him to pray earnestly for Jacob and his team. In Phuah's words:

I remember seeing a beach scene where people were running helter-skelter due to the presence of police. Some stood still, but Jacob and two others were hiding behind a rock and there was water around their feet. I remember being jolted out of this vision and praying for safety and the covering of God to be upon these faithful men. I prayed that the authorities would not see them and that no one would suffer any harassment during the search.

The police finally left, taking with them a few of the local leaders for three more hours of questioning. Eventually, they were released. The police had been searching for any foreigners in the meeting, and the presence of a non-Chinese leader would have been problematic, to say the least. After the police had left, two of the Chinese leaders went to the group hiding behind the big rock, brought them back to the hotel, helped them pack their bags, and transferred them to another hotel. They flew out of China safely the next morning.

When Jacob finally got back to Malaysia and shared what had happened to them, Phuah told him about the vision he had received. The vision and the raid had happened at the same time.

7. Prayer and God's Protection. In response to the September 11, 2001 attack on the World Trade Center in New York, U.S. and coalition forces from other nations invaded Afghanistan in October 2001. After two years of fighting the Taliban, the coalition forces were able to secure Kabul and most of Afghanistan. When a window of opportunity opened in 2003 for missionaries to enter Kabul, Every Nation teams from Asia, Europe, and the United States were eager to go. Over 100 volunteered from Asia alone, which was far too many. Like Gideon and the armies of Israel, Asian leaders had to cut the number down to seventeen.

March 20, 2003 was the first day of the invasion of Iraq—Operation Enduring Freedom. For this reason, we did not want the teams to proceed to Afghanistan. However, the Asian team, having already landed in Dubai, was given the option to proceed. Since the Americans and the International Security Assistance Force were already set up in Afghanistan, the Asian team chose to go on to Kabul. They arrived on April 6 and began working with a Christian NGO based in Afghanistan and several members of our Every Nation churches in North America who were already there.

Within a week of their arrival, the team set up a clinic in Kabul University and soon established good rapport with the president of the university. Because our team members were all professionals, some manned the clinic while others taught English, engineering, political science, management, information technology, and even driving. This was their way of engaging the local faculty and students at the university. Our missionaries were influencing a lot of Afghan students for Christ.

The team met one of the more influential students who was related to a high-ranking member of the Taliban. As they shared their lives and stories with him, he would share security information with them. Two months into their stay, he warned them that a religious leader (*imam*) had issued a death sentence on our team in Kabul. Visiting intercessors had also warned the team that they should be on their guard. At the same time, both American and British embassies issued warnings that Taliban fighters were planning a four-day bloodbath against coalition forces. This was more than enough to put our team on high alert and motivate them to engage in some serious intercessory prayer. They also had a heightened awareness of the words of the Apostle Paul, "For we do not wrestle against flesh and blood, but against the rulers, against the authorities, against the cosmic powers over this present darkness, against the spiritual forces of evil in the heavenly places" (Ephesians 6:12).

Over the next few weeks, there were numerous attacks by the Taliban, leaving many Afghans and those of the coalition forces dead or wounded. On the third day of the Taliban's campaign, Mel Techo, the leader of the Filipino team, felt the need to pray earnestly for protection. Eventually, the Lord gave him peace and assured him that He was with them. Later that morning, several team members were leaving the compound in Central Kabul for the eight-kilometer trip to the university. In the last van were an Afghan driver, three Americans, one German, and two Filipinos, including Mel.

About three kilometers away from the university, Mel noticed that two men on a motorcycle had aligned with their van. Seconds later, the rider in the back pulled the pin on a Russian fragmentation grenade and threw it into the front passenger window of their van. Russian grenades typically have a twelve-second fuse. The American passenger in the front seat picked it up and asked what it was, to which Mel replied, "It's a grenade." Upon hearing this, he threw the grenade out his window with just a few seconds to spare. Amazingly enough, Mel recalled that he had not panicked when this happened, but only felt God's presence and peace like earlier that morning. Afghan and American security forces later discovered that the Russian grenade did not explode.

The grenade incident changed the attitudes of both students and faculty toward the team. Muslims regard miracles with high esteem, and so they concluded that the hand of God had protected and covered the team that day. Mel helped disciple four students in Afghanistan—the relative of the Taliban leader, two who had recently finished their law studies, and one who now works at the U.S. Library in Kabul University.

GLOBAL MISSIONS CHALLENGE

These stories serve as illustrations of why we must be committed to prayer. Prayer is essential because . . .

. . . perhaps at the critical juncture of a church plant, you desperately need God's favor and protection so that even an unbeliever can intercede on your behalf.

. . . perhaps you find yourself in a situation where you have to make an outrageously bold stand for the gospel.

. . . perhaps your life depends on giving an answer from the Holy Spirit in front of the court.

. . . perhaps securing the meeting place God wants you to have means going back again and again like a crazy person who simply won't take no for an answer.

. . . perhaps the step of faith in front of you requires a boldness that can come only from being filled with the Holy Spirit.

. . . perhaps your safety depends on someone waking up in the middle of the night with an intense burden to pray for you and your team.

I hope you realize that these possibilities and reasons to pray are just as applicable for those in Europe, the Americas, or Oceania as they are for those in Africa, Asia, and the Middle East. The only strategy that can help you in those desperate moments is to bathe every aspect of your endeavor in prayer.

Chapter 10

Give with Generosity

It is beyond the realm of possibilities that one has the ability to out-give God. Even if I give the whole of my worth to Him, He will find a way to give back to me much more than I gave.

—Charles Spurgeon
19th-century Baptist; known as the "Prince of Preachers"

Now the Lord said to Abram, "Go from your country and your kindred and your father's house to the land that I will show you. And I will make of you a great nation, and I will bless you and make your name great, so that you will be a blessing. I will bless those who bless you . . . and in you all the families of the earth shall be blessed."

—Genesis 12:1–3

THE WORD "GO" IS DEEPLY IMPRINTED in the hearts and minds of all missionaries who serve in Every Nation, particularly those whose lives have been defined by that initial step—the willingness to leave everything behind and go in obedience to the Great Commission. In the spirit of the Abrahamic Covenant, they went out by faith, not knowing where they were going (Hebrews 11:8). In other words, many have gone into all the world to make disciples of all nations, and like Abraham they went with a degree of uncertainty about what they were getting themselves into.

"All the world" (Mark 16:15) includes nations that are blessed with great economic prosperity as well as nations that seem to struggle endlessly under the weight of systemic poverty. Many campus ministries and churches in the world probably do not have the resources to become great church-planting movements. That being said, no matter the poverty index or economic stability of your nation, the Great Commission still applies to you and your church. The financial resources of a city or nation do not limit God's purpose and power.

But perhaps what does limit us from becoming church-planting centers is the way we view ourselves, our church, and our nation. Some churches have tried to address this self-perception with a gospel of prosperity, having the faith to **get** without a vision to **go**. When you think about it, this false gospel is just as prevalent in developed countries as it is in developing ones.

What is often missed in the story of Abraham's going is that he was always to go as a blessing, not only to the nation to which he was called, but to all the nations of the world. God's purpose, covenant promise, and calling were that "all the families of the earth shall be blessed" through him (Genesis 12:3). In order to go and actually be a blessing to all nations, we will need a much bigger vision. What follows is how our church in Manila was able to break out of a mission-field mentality to become a missionary-sending church.

VICTORY CHURCH PLANT

In the early days of the initial church plant in 1984, the weekly offerings at Victory U-Belt were quite heavy—because the offering bags were mostly filled with coins from students. One of the students reached at that time recalls those early days: "You could hear the clink of coins as each person gave his or her contribution. As the increasingly heavy bag was passed along, the coins would clink even more. One time I was asked to help count the offering. The table was covered with coins neatly stacked up in rows—one-peso, fifty-centavo, twenty-five-centavo, ten-centavo, and five-centavo coins."

Bishop Ferdie also adds: "My first job as a new believer and member of Victory was to serve as an usher. So we were responsible for taking up the offering. There were a few paper bills from the working professionals, but our church was made up of mostly students. So the offering consisted mostly of coins. To us, however, the collection seemed like a king's ransom, and we guarded it with our lives."

Throughout those early years, we kept preaching the gospel, making disciples, and taking up heavy offerings. However, as we hired more staff members, each was introduced to the pressure of operating a church at a deficit, a reality that was driven home every time we were short on rent money. We would periodically take up offerings among the staff to pay for our rent every month. Our credibility as well as our testimony were at stake. The twelve of us who were on staff would bow our heads, pray, and wait for a number. If the amount collected was insufficient, we had nowhere else to appeal for money. So we did the only thing we knew—we prayed again. This happened on several occasions.

Few people beyond the original staff knew the extent of our periodic shortfalls. The rent, salaries, and other ministry expenses frequently came in ways that even I still cannot explain today. But the miraculous provision rarely occurred apart from sacrificial giving. In those early years, our church could only cover about 65 percent of our monthly budget. God answered our many prayers by adding a few people to our church who had financial resources. A wealthy Chinese businessman and his wife, along with their daughter, became part of Victory U-Belt. He was a hard worker who owned several restaurants and led a large financial institution in the Philippines. In a service filled with wild, worshiping young people on fire for Jesus, two people never looked more out-of-place than they did. The gentleman would typically fold his arms across his chest and sleep through most of the services. But they really loved us, and their regular offerings covered about 40 percent of our budget. The gentleman has since gone on to be with the Lord, and I trust that they will reap the rewards of what they have sown. We would have liked a dozen generous givers like them in our church, but that was not the prayer God answered nor the lesson He was trying to teach us.

FIRST TO GO

I have the privilege of being the first staff member of our young church, and the first Filipino to be ordained as a Victory pastor. As such, one of my first ministry assignments was to serve as the missions director—a job I've loved for over thirty years. During the time of small beginnings, however, there really wasn't much to direct. Nonetheless, we were so inspired and challenged by the vision of the American missionaries who had reached out to us that for the next two years we engaged in missions locally. We sent a team to a province south of Manila (about an eight-hour bus ride). We simply did what we had seen the Americans do in 1984: We engaged the local people of the community through mime, skits, and songs. We preached the gospel, and the majority received Jesus as their Lord and

Savior. We were surprised to see that God could actually use us to make a difference in the community.

In 1986, we sent out our first international short-term missions team to the nation of Indonesia. Jerry Santiago, Noel Manayon, Emily Tuy, and Gigi Lim (who is now my wife) began engaging students in campus outreaches to help a new church plant in Jakarta. This first exposure to cross-cultural missions triggered an avalanche of excitement at Victory. It was soon followed by another short-term mission trip to Japan. Our little church was actually going into all the world, participating in the Great Commission. I remember the feeling—as if we were living out the book of Acts. And it was happening through us, just as Pastor Steve had said it would.

The feeling in the air at Victory was that anything was possible for those who dared to believe—but our passion still needed provision. We were quickly coming to realize that international missions takes money, and a lot of it. You'd think that we would have figured that out before the two-year mark at Victory. However, many of us had grown up with a poverty mentality. I had been one of the many who came to Metro Manila to pursue a better opportunity, and I felt like this idea of always looking to our own needs was more prevalent for us, since this was all we had ever known. I had recently graduated from college, and we were just a handful of young professionals in church. Contrary to this perception that seemed normal to us in a developing nation, almost every pastor coming through Manila made bold declarations—often punctuated with a "thus sayeth the Lord!"—that we would become a missionary-sending church and a launching pad for the gospel to be preached in the rest of Asia. Everyone would rejoice and shout, "Amen!" But since we had no clue how that could ever happen, most of us would revert to our old way of thinking that we needed to receive more than we could actually give. To be honest, we had faith to believe for almost anything—as long as it didn't involve money.

FROM A FIELD NATION TO A SOWING NATION

Pastor Steve, who came with the original team and stayed when they all left, didn't have much money either. He and his wife, Deborah, had only thought they would be in Manila for one month. However, that one month turned into two, then four, then six—for the next thirty-five years. There had been no time to assemble a team of financial partners from the U.S. to fund their efforts in the Philippines. The church was growing, and though Pastor Steve and Deborah didn't have much more resources than we did, they had faith and a vision that God would provide and make us into a missionary-sending church. That's why he would always tell us that as new believers, we needed both a Bible and a passport—a Bible to know God and a passport to obey Him. Although it took a couple of years for us to catch up with this faith and vision, it has been ingrained in me ever since.

Eventually, we were filled with passion and vision, and we had leaders who were ready to go. We just needed to change the way we were thinking—from considering our needs as a nation to being a blessing to the nations of the world. This venture would require great faith, since fulfilling our vision was going to be very expensive.

I remember the day in 1986 when Pastor Steve shared with the staff his vision for sowing into the nations. He said, "The sowers scatter their seed among the fields, and in time they go out to reap a harvest. But the fields never reap the harvest; the sowers do. If we want to reap a harvest among the nations of the world, we need to be sowing into those nations."

Those who consider themselves to be a poor and needy mission field often think they are blessed when they are able to convince churches in more developed nations to support them. In some ways they are correct. However, it's not the mission field that receives the blessing, it's the sowers who are "more blessed." Jesus said, "It is more blessed to give than to receive" (Acts 20:35).

Perhaps there were some skeptical "yeah-buts" and "what-ifs" among the staff. Most of us still thought of ourselves as a mission field in the developing world that needed sowing into. However, listening to Pastor Steve made my heart burn with a word from the Holy Spirit aimed directly at me. Not only were we to begin sowing into the nations, this was also God's way of breaking us out of a poverty mentality.

Shortly after, Pastor Steve presented a plan for the entire church to give to missions. At that time Victory consisted of about 350 people, mostly students meeting in the Tandem Theater basement in Metro Manila's U-Belt. He challenged the church to make a monthly pledge to missions—funds that would only be used to support missionary efforts around the world. These pledges would be given over and above regular tithes and offerings. They could not be pledges that required some kind of miracle to obtain. We intended to make commitments to individual missionaries and mission initiatives, so the pledges needed to be a part of our budgeted expenses.

As Pastor Steve shared the challenge, I was thinking: *With all those restrictions and the limited resources of our student congregation, will anyone respond at all?* But oh me of little faith! Our church responded with overwhelming enthusiasm. Pastor Steve and the other leaders had been casting a vision for two years among the new believers, trying to instill the vision for world missions and the faith to believe that they could be participants in the Great Commission. It was as if that vision for missions had finally found its release.

Though some students pledged as little as PHP 10, almost every Victory member got involved. The total monthly pledge amounted to well over PHP 10,000, but almost completely in coins that filled the offering bags. Since the Philippines was in the middle of a revolution that eventually toppled the presidency of Ferdinand Marcos, our economy was unstable and sent the peso into a free fall. Though everyone gave with all the faith and generosity they could muster, the pledges amounted to only a little over USD 200 today. I look back at that now as a seed that God planted in our hearts and in the nations of the world.

MISSION PLEDGES OVER THE YEARS

With our combined sacrificial pledges amounting to USD 200 per month, we made commitments to give to missionaries in Japan, Latin America, and South Africa. For over three decades, our churches throughout the Philippines have made giving to missions a priority. In the parable of the sower and the soils, Jesus made a reference to seeds that bore fruit at thirty, sixty, and a hundredfold. Since then, our monthly pledges exclusively for international missions have increased 650 times. In the last five years alone, Victory Manila's missions pledges have increased at an average rate of 20 percent per year.

I think I can hear what you're thinking as I write this. Victory has grown significantly in over three decades. Naturally, our giving has greatly increased as well. However, this is not simply a natural thing. Giving to missions in our churches has never been about setting aside a percentage of the general offering. We couldn't afford that in 1986 because our offerings just barely covered expenses, and sometimes fell even short of that. Regardless of whether or not we could afford to support international missions out of the general fund (then or now), it was far more important to us that individual members would have the opportunity to directly participate in global missions initiatives. In other words, they needed to be personally involved in giving specifically to missions.

Unfortunately, as churches get older and larger, the founders' vision for evangelism, meaningful discipleship, and cross-cultural missions can wane. Some of that might be considered the natural course of church growth—being more community-minded, less focused on discipleship, and less committed to participating in the Great Commission by praying, giving, and going. Nevertheless, our calling is to be more spiritually-minded than naturally-minded. As believers, we are, in the words of the Apostle Paul, to "set your minds on things that are above, not on things that are on earth. For you have died, and your life is hidden with Christ in God" (Colossians 3:2,3).

Tracking missionary giving from individual members is like taking the spiritual temperature of the church. In the same way that Victory measures ministry success primarily in terms of water baptisms and small group leaders rather than worship service attendance, the number of missionary pledges over and above the tithes is a barometer of the congregation's commitment to the Great Commission. As someone who has led our missions efforts in the last three decades, I find it amazing that the percentage of members who make annual pledges to missions has kept pace with our church growth.

With that in mind, here are some key factors to sustaining giving to missions, both for individual missionaries and ministry initiatives.

By casting the vision and rallying the church, individual pledges to global missions can continue increasing through the years. At Victory, members have continued to make pledges over the years as we upgraded our efforts to promote the vision for giving to international missions.

Here are some of the things we do:

↗ Every October since 1986 has been designated as the time we renew our missions pledges, and the pastors and staff are the first to make these commitments.

↗ We don't just rely on announcements or public appeals to be involved in missions; we spend several weeks prior to the annual offering meeting with key missions partners. We are able to give them updates that we cannot always share publicly. These meetings and regular updates have helped increase giving to missions.

↗ Then, for two consecutive Sundays, church members are invited to continue or make new pledges. The parameters have remained unchanged—funds can only be used for initiatives outside the Philippines, they are given above and beyond the tithes and offerings to the local church, and they can't be pledges that require some kind of miracle to obtain.

↗ On the first weekend of each month, Victory churches throughout the Philippines collect those missions pledges. It's worth noting that Victory pastors are not trying to raise money for international missions initiatives every first weekend. They're simply collecting funds that have already been pledged. This is similar to what the Apostle Paul wrote regarding the offering he intended to collect for the church in Jerusalem: "On the first day of every week, each of you is to put something aside and store it up, as he may prosper, so that there will be no collecting when I come" (1 Corinthians 16:2). Since 2008, we have been showing video updates for a particular nation or region at worship services on the first weekend of every month. We also use special envelopes designed for missions giving. These serve as a gentle reminder.

Our churches in Manila and throughout the Philippines are very intentional about promoting and sustaining a culture of giving to missions. We do this because we know that it's easy for our commitments to fall by the wayside. After all, out of sight, out of mind. We believe that the passion for giving to missions will continue to burn in our hearts only if we continue to fan the flames.

The spiritual foundation imparted from the beginning largely determines how successfully you can build on it. We have constantly evaluated and tweaked every aspect of the discipleship journey. However, some things never changed. We still talk about the Great Commission and needing a Bible and a passport in every *Victory Weekend* and foundations class. Bishop Ferdie relates a story from one *Victory Weekend* many years ago:

> At the close of the weekend retreat, I decided to bring them out to an open field. Since we were 80 km outside Manila, the night was clear and the stars had never been brighter. I asked them to lie down, look up at the heavens, and try to estimate how many stars they could see from one horizon to another . . . God had done the same thing with Abram. ". . . Then he said to him, 'So shall your offspring be'" (Genesis 15:4–6). God was trying to expand Abram's vision concerning the promises being made to him so that he would not limit what God wanted to do through him by his lack of faith.
>
> . . . After a few minutes, I told the group of teenagers to stand. "You cannot count the stars," I said, "but I want you to dream, and dream big. I want you to have a vision of God's future and His plan for you. I want you to see yourself making an impact in your generation for Christ with His power. I want you to begin seeing yourselves as leaders of multitudes."
>
> Many of those visionary teenagers are now leaders in Victory.[1]

Here's the good and bad news for pastors and missionary church planters. If you lay that foundation and consistently build upon it, you'll never have a problem inspiring your church members to pray, give, or go to international missions. That's the good news. On the other hand, if you allow your congregation to outgrow that vision and commitment to the Great Commission, it will be very difficult to regain it. In some cases, it may even be impossible, and might only be regained within a small group in the church. It is so much easier to keep a fire burning than to restart it with a pile of wet wood.

Sustaining the vision for a missionary-sending church is possible, but only to the extent that it burns in the heart of the senior leader. Unless senior pastors are committed to being apostolic churches that regularly challenge their congregations to obey the Great Commission, this level of missionary giving will never happen. This is not a responsibility that can be delegated to a staff member. The ongoing participation in global missions outside the Philippines is **only possible** because of Pastor Steve, Bishop Ferdie, and other senior pastors across the Philippines. They have bought into the vision of sowing generously into the nations by giving to churches and missionaries outside the Philippines.

As the former missions director and now the Asia Leadership Team director for Every Nation, I'm merely riding on the momentum of our senior pastors' apostolic vision. In fact, global missions is so much a part of our church culture that upcoming leaders are unlikely to become senior pastors without having embraced that vision.

GLOBAL MISSIONS CHALLENGE

In every church plant with which I've been involved, whether locally or internationally, I say to new believers at the beginning, "Right now, God is using us Filipinos to go and preach the gospel to you. Very soon the day will come when you will go to other nations. You're going to bring the gospel to them just as we have brought it to you, so read your Bible and get a passport."

The first challenge for missionary church planters to build a culture of generosity is to instill that same vision and accept the personal responsibility of perpetually maintaining it. The senior leader has to effectively carry the vision and burden for the Great Commission.

The second challenge is to invite the church to begin giving generously to global missions. It took two years for our church to break the stronghold of poverty mentality and give beyond our capacity. This generosity radically changed our perception from looking to our own needs to giving to the nations.

Chapter 11

Go with Tenacity

Meanwhile the holy apostles and disciples of our Savior were dispersed throughout the world. Parthia, according to tradition, was allotted to Thomas as his field of labor, Scythia to Andrew, and Asia to John, who, after he had lived some time there, died in Ephesus. Peter appears to have preached in Pontus, Galatia, Bithynia, Cappadocia, and Asia to the Jews of the dispersion. At the last, having come to Rome, he was crucified head-downwards; for he had requested that he might suffer in this way. What do we need to say concerning Paul, who preached the Gospel of Christ from Jerusalem to Illyricum, and afterwards suffered martyrdom in Rome under Nero? These facts are related by Origen in the third volume of his Commentary on Genesis.

—Eusebius Pamphili (AD 263–339)
Author, *Historia Ecclesiastica*

And Jesus came and said to them, "All authority in heaven and on earth has been given to me. Go therefore and make disciples of all nations, baptizing them in the name of the Father and of the Son and of the Holy Spirit, teaching them to observe all that I have commanded you. And behold, I am with you always, to the end of the age."

—Matthew 28:18–20

THE MOST RELIABLE INFORMATION on the going of the twelve apostles is found in the writing of those who lived during their lifetimes—Flavius Josephus (AD 37–100) who recorded Jewish history with special emphasis on the first century and the life of Jesus—as well as those who lived close to their lifetimes: Eusebius Pamphili, the Bishop of Caesarea (AD 263–339), and Hippolytus of Rome (AD 170–235). From those accounts, Dr. Anthony Mariot, a research writer and lecturer on Biblical Antiquity at Oxford University, provides a summary of the missionary endeavors of the twelve apostles.

↗ Andrew, the brother of Peter, went as a missionary to the Scythians (Georgia) and Thracians (Bulgaria) and was crucified and buried at Patrae, a town of Achaia (Greece).

↗ Bartholomew (also known as Nathanael) went as a missionary to India, possibly preaching the gospel in Turkey, Iraq, Iran, Afghanistan, and/or Pakistan on his way to India where he was finally crucified upside down and buried in Allanum.

↗ James, Son of Alphaeus, became a local missionary and was stoned to death by the Jews in Jerusalem while preaching. He was buried there beside the temple.

↗ James, one of the two sons of Zebedee, was also a local missionary in Judea who was beheaded by Herod in Judea (Acts 12:1,2).

↗ John the Beloved, the other son of Zebedee, went to Asia Minor. He was banished to the Isle of Patmos by the Emperor Domitian and later died of old age in Ephesus.

↗ Matthew (or Levi) went as a missionary to Parthia (Iran) and died of old age in the town of Hierees near modern-day Tehran.

↗ Peter was a missionary to Pontus, Galatia, Cappadocia (regions of modern-day Turkey), Betania, Italy, and Asia. He was crucified upside down in Rome by the Emperor Nero.

↗ Philip (not to be confused with Philip, one of the seven deacons in Acts 6:5) went as a missionary to Phrygia (Turkey) where he was crucified upside down in Hierapolis.

↗ Simon the Zealot preached the gospel in Jerusalem, where he became the city's second bishop after the martyrdom of James the Just. Simon died in his sleep and was buried there.

↗ Thaddaeus went as a missionary to Edessa and to the surrounding Mesopotamian region (Iraq, Syria, Turkey, Iran). He died at Berytus (modern-day Beirut) and was buried there.

↗ Thomas went as a missionary to the Parthians, Medes, Persians, and Hyrcanians (Iran), the Bactrians (Afghanistan), and Margians (Afghanistan). He eventually made his way to India, where he was thrust through in the four members of his body with a pine spear at the city of Calamene.

↗ Matthias (chosen to replace Judas in Acts 1:21–26) was a local missionary in Jerusalem who died of old age.

↗ Paul went as a missionary to the west as far as the provinces of Illyricum (Croatia), Italy, and possibly to Spain. He was beheaded in Rome by Nero.[1]

Out of the fourteen (counting Matthias and Paul), one was lost forever, four became local missionaries in Jerusalem and Judea, and nine went to the regions beyond. Eight were martyred for their faith. James, the brother of Jesus, became the patriarch of Jerusalem as, one by one, the apostles left to spread the gospel and plant churches.

BEYOND THE TWELVE

The twelve apostles mentioned in the New Testament have a unique place both in the history of the church and the eternal kingdom. Jesus said of the twelve, "Truly, I say to you, in the new world, when the Son of Man will sit on his glorious throne, you who have followed me will also sit on twelve thrones, judging the twelve tribes of Israel" (Matthew 19:28). Of the heavenly city He said, "And the wall of the city had twelve foundations, and on them were the twelve names of the twelve apostles of the Lamb" (Revelation 21:14). There are other apostles and prophets mentioned in the New Testament. However, the reference to apostles and prophets as being the foundation of the church (Ephesians 2:20) refers specifically to the twelve apostles and the Old Testament prophets—not contemporary ministers with apostolic or prophetic giftings.

That being said, there were many more who Jesus personally appointed and sent out as His apostles. Note that the Greek word *apóstolos* simply means a messenger, or one who is sent. Jesus appointed seventy (some manuscripts say seventy-two) and "sent them on ahead of him . . . into every town and place where he himself was about to go" (Luke 10:1). These were not merely public relations front-men. They were empowered as apostolic messengers. The after-engagement report of the seventy was:

"'Lord, even the demons are subject to us in your name!' And he said to them, 'I saw Satan fall like lightning from heaven'" (Luke 10:17,18).

So, who were these seventy "sent ones"? Several lists were constructed in the early days of the church, some of which still exist. Hippolytus of Rome made a list of the seventy from his own sources. He was strongly influenced by Irenaeus (circa AD 130–200), who was a disciple of Polycarp (AD 69–156), who was in turn a disciple of the Apostle John. The list of Hippolytus is a small work entitled *On the Seventy Apostles of Christ.*[2] The document appears in the appendix of a collection of writings of early church fathers and includes James, the Lord's brother; Agabus, the prophet (Acts 11:28; 21:10); Mark and Luke, the authors of two Gospels; Barnabas; Stephen and Philip along with the five other deacons (Acts 6:1–6); and many other individuals mentioned in the New Testament. The authenticity of this entire list, whether or not it actually originated with Hippolytus, is not universally accepted. What is without doubt, however, is that Jesus sent out other individuals as His apostles. Imagine the impact of the seventy along with the twelve, empowered by the Holy Spirit, sent out in every direction to make disciples of all nations.

Two of the seven deacons appointed to serve the widows in Jerusalem were Stephen and Philip. They did a lot more than wait on tables; they played a vital role in the spread of the early church. The martyrdom of Stephen (Acts 7:54–60) and the subsequent systematic persecution led by Saul of Tarsus scattered the seeds of the gospel throughout Judea and Samaria while the apostles remained in Jerusalem. Philip went to Samaria, preached the gospel with signs and wonders, and birthed a great revival there (Acts 8:4–25). He left the Samaritan revival and went to the desert road that led from Jerusalem to Gaza. There he met an Ethiopian official returning from Jerusalem and led him to faith in Christ. That was the seed that became the Ethiopian church today. Other believers, fleeing the persecution of Saul, made their way to Phoenicia and Cyprus, and to Antioch where believers were first called Christians (Acts 11:19–26). This was where Saul, the converted persecutor of the church, began his missionary journeys.

TWENTY CENTURIES OF GOING

That was only the beginning of missionaries going into all the world to make disciples for Christ. Throughout the last twenty centuries since the

Resurrection, missionaries have been going. Sometimes they have been propelled by powerful missionary movements and have gone by the tens of thousands to engage the world for Christ. In other seasons when the church became inwardly oriented, the number of those going dwindled and became a trickle. But there has never been a time when there was no one willing to forsake all to go to the remotest parts of the world, preaching the gospel of Jesus Christ and making disciples of all nations. Missionaries have continued to go throughout the twenty centuries of the church. Below are just a few examples, punctuated by historical facts and events.

In AD 70, the Roman general Titus destroys Jerusalem, and Antioch subsequently becomes one of the centers of Christianity in the eastern half of the Roman Empire.

AD 180—Pantaenus goes to India. Pantaenus was a Stoic philosopher and a native of Sicily teaching in Alexandria. He became a Christian and an apologist, reconciling his new faith with Greek philosophy. Eusebius writes in *Historia Ecclesiastica*, "[Pantaenus] displayed such zeal for the divine Word, that he was appointed as a herald of the Gospel of Christ to the nations in the East, and was sent as far as India." There he preached "Christ to the Brahmans and philosophers," and found Christian communities using the Gospel of Matthew written in the "Hebrew language," left to them supposedly by the Apostle Bartholomew.[3]

By AD 200, six generations after the resurrection of Jesus, an estimated 0.11 percent of the world's population is Christian.[4]

AD 258—Dionysius goes to France. Gregory of Tours writes, "Of all the Roman missionaries sent into Gaul, Dionysius carried the faith the furthest into the country." He established regional church centers at Paris and (along with his disciples) the churches in Chartres, Meaux, Senlis, Cologne, and others. Together they brought "great numbers to the faith." The pagan priests were threatened by their many conversions, and Dionysius and his disciples were beheaded on Montmartre, or "The Martyr's Mountain."[5]

AD 350—Frumentius goes to Ethiopia. As a young Christian, Frumentius was captured and taken as a slave to Ethiopia, where he gained favor and became the treasurer and secretary of the king. As an official, he persuaded Christian businessmen to come to Ethiopia and secured freedom of worship for Christians. When the king died, Frumentius was released and allowed to return to Alexandria where he reported on the Christian presence in Ethiopia. Bishop Athanasius sent him back to Ethiopia as a missionary for Christ. Although he died around AD 380 with much of the country yet to become Christian, Frumentius is regarded as the apostle to Ethiopia.

In AD 375, over 7,000 Christian monks[6] are in established and flourishing monasteries in Egypt, and about 15 percent of the world's population is Christian.[7]

AD 432—Patrick goes to Ireland. According to the *Confession of Saint Patrick*, at the age of sixteen he was captured by a group of Irish pirates. They took him to Ireland where he was enslaved and held captive for six years. While in captivity, he worked as a shepherd and strengthened his relationship with God through prayer, eventually leading him to convert to Christianity. After six years in captivity, he heard a voice telling him that he would soon go home and that his ship was ready. Fleeing his master, he travelled to a port 200 miles away, where he found a ship and with difficulty persuaded the captain to take him in. Patrick recounts that he had a vision a few years after returning home:

> I saw a man coming, as it were from Ireland. His name was Victoricus, and he carried many letters, and he gave me one of them. I read the heading: "The Voice of the Irish." As I began the letter, I imagined in that moment that I heard the voice of those very people who were near the wood of Foclut, which is beside the western sea— and they cried out, as with one voice: "We appeal to you, holy servant boy, to come and walk among us."[8]

Acting on his vision, Patrick returned to Ireland as a Christian missionary. For over thirty years he contended with pagans who tried to kill him, baptized thousands of converts (including members of the Irish nobility), and ordained leaders of the new Christian communities. Patrick was not only the apostle to the Irish but probably history's most effective Christian missionary.

By AD 500, almost 20 percent of the world embraces Christianity (63 percent nonwhite).[9] There are over 2,000,000 known martyrs since the birth of the church.[10]

AD 563—Columba goes to Scotland. Born of a noble family in Donegal, Ireland, Columba took his monastic vows as a young man and fulfilled them with extraordinary passion. He is attributed with founding twenty-five monasteries and forty churches. At the age of forty-two, Columba began missions. With twelve others, he sailed to Iona (modern-day Britain). From there he carried out missions to the Picts and the Scots, who were two major tribes on the mainland, and to the northern English communities. Columba is credited with planting Celtic churches in Scotland that were independent of Rome.

AD 635—Alopen goes to China. The Nestorian Stele was a stone monument erected near Chang'an, China, around AD 781, chronicling almost 150 years of Christianity in China—beginning with the arrival of Alopen and the first missionaries who formed the Nestorian churches of Syria. T'ai-tsung, the reigning monarch, welcomed Alopen and arranged for the translation of the holy writings he had brought with him at the Imperial Library. Three years later, T'ai-tsung built the first Christian church in China and recognized twenty-one priests. Alopen held a position similar to a bishop over the many churches established throughout China. The Nestorian church in China disappeared from recorded history in the early tenth century as a result of persecution, but was reintroduced by the Mongols. When the Nestorian Stele was discovered in the seventeenth century, the Chinese were surprised to find that the "new" religion being preached by the missionaries had actually been in existence in China for more than ten centuries.

AD 722—Boniface goes to Friesland. When Boniface (formerly Wynfrith) was five, missionary monks visited his family, which was of the nobility in Wessex, England. Since then, he decided he wanted to be a traveling evangelist and become a Benedictine monk, despite his parents' secular preferences for him. When he was in his early forties, he went to Friesland (the northern Netherlands) for missions. A Frisian revolution forced him to go home without having baptized anyone. Not to be dissuaded from his missionary calling, he traveled to Rome, where Pope Gregory II gave him a new name—Boniface (meaning good works). Gregory II commented, "You seem to glow with the salvation-bringing fire which our Lord came to send upon the earth."[11] Boniface went back to Friesland, evangelizing, baptizing, establishing monasteries and churches, opposing heresy, destroying idols, and challenging "ambitious and free-living clerics" until he was appointed as archbishop of Mainz in Germany. In his late seventies, Boniface resigned from his position and went back to Friesland, traveling the country while baptizing new Christians and building churches for them. As is the case with those driven by a missionary zeal, Boniface could be difficult and was at times extreme and tactless. He was killed by a band of pagan raiders in AD 754. From the eighth to the eleventh century, he became one of the missionaries' top role models.

AD 781 is the peak of Nestorian Christian influence in China, documented by a nine-foot stone (the Nestorian Stele) discovered near Chang'an by workmen in 1623.

AD 863—Cyril and Methodius go to Moravia. A prince of Moravia, Rastislav, asked the Byzantine emperor, Michael III, to send missionaries "to explain to us the Christian truths in our own language."[12] The emperor sent them the brothers Cyril and Methodius, who were known teachers and administrators. Cyril and Methodius returned home because of international politics, and Cyril died in Rome. Methodius travelled back to Moravia to continue their work, but was accused of overstepping his authority and of the "scandalous use of the Slavonic language" in the liturgy.[13] However, in their lifetimes, the Eastern Orthodox Church recognized and acknowledged this great missionary team.

AD 934—Haakon Haraldsson goes to Norway. Haakon the Good was the king of Norway from AD 934 to 961. He had been sent to England for his education and protection, where he learned about Christianity. Upon his return to Norway, Haakon was the first to try to evangelize the Norwegians. However, his efforts were met with stiff opposition from pagan leaders. Later, missionaries from England and Germany also came to preach the gospel in Norway, meeting the same opposition as Haakon had among the people. But the king at that time, Olaf I, was converted to Christianity. A later king, Olaf II, successfully brought Christianity to Norway. Multiple times before the 1900s, Norway held the record for sending more missionaries per capita than any other country.[14]

Circa 1000—Leif Eriksson returns to Greenland. Leif Eriksson was the younger son of Erik the Red, who first settled in Greenland. Eriksson was supposedly the first European in North America, 500 years before Christopher Columbus. Around the year 1000, Eriksson sailed from Greenland to Norway, where he served in the court of King Olaf I and was converted from Norse paganism to Christianity. Soon thereafter, Olaf commissioned Eriksson to spread Christianity to the settlers of Greenland. Thjodhild, Lief Eriksson's mother, was one of the first new Christians in Greenland. She built the first Christian church where Erik the Red had founded his settlement.

In 1000, Nestorian Christians comprise a significant part of the population of Iraq, as well as Khorasan and Syria (both parts of modern-day Iran and Afghanistan).

1124—Otto of Bamberg goes to Pomerania. At that time, Pomerania (Bavaria) was almost completely non-Christian. For more than a century, Pomeranians had lived in a state of constant warfare with their Polish neighbors. Each successive invasion of their country was followed by compulsory baptism. Not surprisingly, Christianity was regarded as the religion of their conquerors and made little progress among them. In 1121, the Duke of Poland Boleslav III announced his intention of converting all the inhabitants to the Christian faith and of destroying them in the event of their refusal. It was at his invitation that Otto, the bishop of the Bamberg diocese, undertook his first missionary journey to Pomerania in 1124. Though physical force was almost always at his disposal, Otto never made use of it, neither to protect himself from being murdered nor to enforce the acceptance of his preaching. Two examples of Otto's power and influence in preaching were in the cities of Pyritz and Stettin. After twenty days of instruction and preparation, Otto baptized 7,000 converts at Pyritz. At Stettin, he remained for three months and left behind 22,156 men who had been baptized. These achievements eventually gave Otto the title of apostle of Pomerania, marking one of the most distinctive stories of the evangelization of Europe.

In 1266, Kublai Khan requests 100 Christian missionaries to be sent to Mongolia. Only two respond but turn back before reaching Mongol territory.[15]

1292—Raymond Lull of Penafort goes to Tunis. Lull had spent nine years studying philosophy as well as Hebrew and Islamic theology. At fifty-six, he went alone on his first missionary journey to the western center of the Muslim world. Because of his passion to preach the gospel to Muslims, he responded to the challenge of the Grand Mufti of Bugia: "If you hold that the law of Christ is true and that of Mohammed false, you must prove it by necessary reasons." Through logic and reasoning, Raymond Lull engaged Muslims both privately and publicly. Lull's strategy: "Missionaries will convert the world by preaching, but also through the shedding of tears and blood and with great labor, and through a bitter death."[16] He went back and forth over Europe, urging political and religious leaders to create schools that would send missionaries to Muslim nations. It was he who urged Thomas Aquinas to prepare definitive arguments that the Dominican missionaries could use in reasoning with the Islamic philosophers. It was at his suggestion that Aquinas prepared his vast *Summa contra Gentiles* (Compendium against the Gentiles). Lull went on three missions to the Muslims, the last when he was in his nineties. In one of his regular public discussions, he started to preach about God's love for all men through Jesus Christ. Those listening were angered, dragged him outside the city, and stoned him to death.

In 1310, there is a large Christian population in Persia, but rulers are still undecided between Christianity and Islam. In the fourteenth century, the Mongol dynasty embraces Islam.

In 1347, there is an outbreak of the Black Death (bubonic plague) that kills an estimated 100 million people, reducing the world's population by almost 25 percent.

1379—Stephen goes to the Perm. Stephen was a missionary to the Zyrians, inhabitants of a region west of the Ural Mountains of Russia. When he was young, Stephen studied Greek in the monastery of St. Gregory the Theologian so he could read the original Scriptures. As he had been raised with the non-believing Zyrians, he wanted to preach the gospel to them. For the next seventeen years Stephen lived among them, and was slowly able to lead many of them to Christ. As Stephen's disciples increased in number, he was named the first bishop of Perm. Eventually, Stephen built churches for the growing congregations, and urged people to open schools beside them. The schools trained future deacons and priests in the Scriptures. The growing number of churches and monasteries Stephen built or encouraged found their clergy in these students. Stephen of Perm is celebrated as the apostle to the Zyrians.

In the 1450s, Johannes Gutenberg prints an edition of the Latin Vulgate using movable type. By 1500 there are over 2,000 printing presses all over Europe, printing a number of materials including Christian books and Bibles.[17]

1491—Dominican and Franciscan missionaries go to the Congo. There is evidence of Christianity in the Congo as early as the late fifteenth century. King Nzinga met Portuguese explorers and became a Christian, renaming himself João. A later king, Afonso I (1506–1543), studied Christian theology in Europe. Today, Christianity is professed by a majority of the population of the Democratic Republic of the Congo. There are over sixty-three million Christians of all denominations in the Congo covering 95.7 percent of the population and 2.9 percent of the global Christian population, according to the Pew Research Center.[18]

In 1517, Martin Luther nails his Ninety-Five Theses to the door of the Wittenberg Castle Church. Many consider this to be the beginning of the Protestant Reformation.

1542—Francis Xavier goes to India. Xavier was a missionary who was chosen to go to India at the behest of the Portuguese king. He learned the different languages and began to preach to the people. He also translated both the Apostles' Creed and the catechism. This strategy was successful, as Jesuits baptized thousands in less than twenty years. Xavier did not stay in India; he also traveled around Asia. In 1549, he traveled to Japan and encountered open doors because of the favor of political leaders. In just a few years, thousands were baptized, and Nagasaki became a central city to the spread of Christianity in Japan.

In 1600 the world population is 18.4 percent Christian and now 91 percent European. In AD 500, the world population was almost 20 percent Christian but predominantly nonwhite.[19]

1619—Alexandre de Rhodes goes to Vietnam. De Rhodes was the first French missionary to Vietnam. He established a mission and was allowed to preach the gospel and make disciples. By his own estimation, he had converted some 6,700 Vietnamese to Christianity. But eleven years later, city leaders became jealous of his following and anticipated that Christianity might challenge sovereign authority, which was based on Confucianism. They threw de Rhodes out of the country. After ten years in Macau, de Rhodes returned to Vietnam, where he continued his missionary work until he was condemned to death in 1646. However, his sentence was reduced to permanent exile. He died in 1660 at the age of sixty-nine while serving as a missionary to Persia.

By 1700, Evangelical Christianity begins to grow rapidly in the developing world, with over 15 million baptized Christians by 1700, over 25 million by 1800, over 95 million by 1900, and 1.2 billion by 2005.[20]

1793—William Carey goes to India. William Carey made quite an impression at his first Northampton ministers' association. Without hesitation Carey spoke up and challenged the members about the responsibility of all Christians to bring the gospel to the ends of the earth. In a subsequent meeting one of the society members commented, "There is a gold mine in India, but it seems almost as deep as the center of the earth."[21] After a time of discussion, another member, Reynold Hogg, asked, "Who will venture down to explore it?" William Carey replied, "I will venture to go down, but remember that you—[Fuller, Sutcliff, and Ryland]—must hold the ropes!"[22]

Carey was on missions in India for forty-one consecutive years. While he only baptized 700 Indians out of millions, any missionaries who followed would find that he had left Bible translations, Bible-based education, and social reforms. His mission endeavors in India, along with those of the British Missionary Society, are commonly cited as the birth of the Modern Missions Movement.

1885—The Cambridge Seven go to China. Seven Cambridge University students volunteered to serve with Hudson Taylor's China Inland Mission, despite being from distinguished British families. Before they left for China, the seven spoke on campuses in England and Scotland, sharing their testimonies and seeing hundreds converted every night.

1963—Bruce Olson goes to Colombia. Bruce Olson, a brilliant nineteen-year-old college dropout already semi-fluent in four languages and a Minnesota Lutheran, bought a one-way ticket to Latin America. Without support from any missions agency, he eventually made his way deep into the Amazonian jungle of Colombia to be the first missionary to the primitive Motilones. The Motilone tribe had lived in that extremely remote area for probably 5,000 years without contact with the outside world. Olson, now in his seventies, had been with the Motilones for almost six decades. He had spent much of his life under threat from communist guerilla groups. He had been kidnapped twice, bitten by extremely poisonous snakes, and shot with arrows or bullets on several occasions. Today, over 70 percent of the Motilone-Bari jungle tribes are Christian disciples. Scores of Motilone-Bari youth have attended university, and, without exception, have returned to the jungle tribes. Some worked as agriculturalists to improve their way of life, while others became lawyers who worked in the legal system to defend the Motilone-Bari land against developers. Olson still operates as a missionary without any ties to a missionary-sending organization. His strategy to reach the Motilone tribe is one of the most effective in evangelical missions to date.

EVERY NATION PERSPECTIVE

Every Nation has been making disciples, training leaders, and sending out cross-cultural missionaries for only a few decades. That's barely a blip on the radar screen of Christian history. Currently we have 419 cross-cultural missionaries in eighty nations—only a small fraction of the 430,000 international missionaries serving somewhere in the world in 2017. The Great Commission is not a competition but a cooperative effort among churches and organizations that have their own unique sense of mission. Some church-planting organizations have focused on a particular nation, region, or people group. Others specialize in various functions of the faith—relief and development, leadership training, or Bible translation. Our movement is called to a special focus as well—planting church-based campus ministries, making disciples, and training leaders in every campus and every nation.

GLOBAL MISSIONS CHALLENGE

Jesus said to His disciples, "'As the Father has sent me, even so I am sending you.' And when he had said this, he breathed on them and said to them, 'Receive the Holy Spirit'" (John 20:21,22).

The Great Commission doesn't begin with us. And though it started with Abram when God promised that in him all the nations of the earth would be blessed (Galatians 3:8), Jesus is the fulfillment of that promise. It was the *missio Dei* (mission of God) from the very beginning.

The challenge to all Christian disciples then is this: What part are you called to play? Will you pray expectantly? Will you give generously? Will you go tenaciously? Perhaps when the Holy Spirit inspires the question in your heart, "Whom shall I send, and who will go for us?" (Isaiah 6:8), your response will be, "Here I am! Send me." And as we respond to this call together and go to the nations, we will see the dream fulfilled of witnessing every tribe, nation, and people bowing to our Lord Jesus Christ:

After this I looked, and behold, a great multitude that no one could number, from every nation, from all tribes and peoples and languages, standing before the throne and before the Lamb, clothed in white robes, with palm branches in their hands, and crying out with a loud voice, "Salvation belongs to our God who sits on the throne, and to the Lamb!"

—Revelation 7:9,10

AFTERWORD

Equip the Next Generation

The key is not to prioritize what's on your schedule, but to schedule your priorities.

—Stephen R. Covey
Author, *The 7 Habits of Highly Effective People*

. . . and what you have heard from me in the presence of many witnesses entrust to faithful men, who will be able to teach others also.

—2 Timothy 2:2

A SENIOR PASTOR'S FOCUS TENDS TO BE FIXED on the squeakiest wheel—the person or the problem demanding the most attention and grease. In any growing congregation, you have new believers in great need of instruction, couples with marital problems who need counseling, volunteers who need training, financial issues that need attention, and people with emotional or spiritual issues who need prayer. It's easy to ignore the ones with no pressing needs. However, a critical concern in any church should be to develop the next wave of missionary church planters.

Jesus was very intentional about ministering to people in need—the sick, the crippled, and the spiritually oppressed. In fact, His ministry could have been completely consumed addressing one problem after another. The continual press of people in need and the occasional extremes they went to in order to get His attention suggests that the public expected Jesus to devote Himself completely to attending to immediate problems. A lot of pastors can probably identify with those expectations.

But that was not His agenda or priority. Jesus did indeed heal and deliver the sick and afflicted; He multiplied the loaves and fish for the hungry. However, **He gave Himself** to His disciples. The priority of His ministry was to the twelve—those whose involvement was defined by their future ministry calling, more than by their immediate needs.

So how does that work practically? For the most part, it happens on three levels.

Jesus regularly spent time explaining the bigger picture. He taught the twelve in the same public meetings that He taught the multitudes, but He was even more deliberate about breaking down the implications privately with that small group (Mark 4:10–12,33,34). Jesus had a special purpose and calling for His immediate disciples: they would be the leaders of the fledgling Christian movement. Spending time with them and explaining things in depth was Jesus' highest priority. It was a deliberate process of **equipping** them for ministry.

Jesus commissioned His disciples by sending them out to speak and minister on His behalf. The essence of **empowerment** is when we entrust upcoming leaders with as much responsibility as they can handle. That was my experience as a young disciple in Victory. Pastor Steve would deliberately and progressively delegate as much responsibility as he could without causing the ministry to run off the tracks. He seemed to be constantly looking to develop the most inexperienced but willing preacher, worship leader, administrator, or small group leader.

We had been Christians for less than two months, and Pastor Steve had us standing on C.M. Recto Avenue, taking turns sharing our salvation stories on the megaphone. We were doing our best to explain what had happened to us in the midst of thousands of angry students marching in the demonstration against President Ferdinand Marcos. Several weeks later, as a way of training young disciples to preach the gospel, Pastor Steve asked four of us to deliver a message in one of our outreach meetings. Three of us exhausted our biblical knowledge in about five minutes, and then the last one came up to make a passionate appeal for other students to receive Christ as their Lord and Savior. That was another new believer, my good friend and now one of Victory's bishops, Ferdie. Through these opportunities, Pastor Steve displayed servant leadership. He willingly stepped back and let us develop our leadership skills.

Jesus was a master at empowering future leaders. He would send them out, bring them back, then talk with them about their victories and challenges. This process is recorded several times in the Gospels, and there were probably many more that we do not know about.

At Victory, we have structured and unstructured times of equipping and internship to help upcoming leaders grow and start their own small groups. We do this through *Making Disciples* and *Empowering Leaders* classes, but also through unscripted discussions that address questions, learning experiences, and problems. These times of impartation do not have an outline or lesson plan, but they are some of the most valuable of all equipping-leadership formats.

THE MAIN THING

Leadership consultant Stephen R. Covey wrote, "The main thing is to keep the main thing the main thing." Over thirty years have come and gone since Victory's early days, but we've worked hard to maintain a culture of empowerment through these kinds of interactions with our next-generation leaders. In Covey's popular management book *The 7 Habits of Highly Effective People*, the third habit is "Put First Things First."[1]

He illustrates the habit by identifying two kinds of responsibilities leaders have to manage (the urgent and the important), which are further broken down into four types. These are: 1) the urgent and important, 2) the not urgent and important, 3) the urgent and not important, 4) the not urgent and not important. Spending quality time with upcoming groups of evangelists, pastors, and missionaries is a responsibility that's not urgent but very important. Focusing on these priorities is not to the exclusion of other responsibilities. Jesus didn't ignore the urgent needs of the multitude, but He put first things first by intentionally giving Himself to the twelve—to mission-focused leadership development.

Putting first things first is a challenge for any senior leader. As the church grows in numbers, if you're not careful, developing future leaders can become a diminished priority. So many things to do, and they all seem so urgent. In such cases, leadership development will take on the character of a staff meeting rather than meaningful personal impartation.

RUNNING WITH THE VISION

As you probably know by now, Every Nation exists to honor God by establishing Christ-centered, Spirit-empowered, socially responsible churches and campus ministries in every nation. Others may be able to explain the heart behind our mission better than I have, and in the future they probably will. Undoubtedly, the greatest lessons from this book are the examples of Every Nation missionaries who have already gone into all the world to win the lost, make disciples, and plant churches. And since they continue to go in increasing numbers from churches being planted all over the world, the greatest stories and the most valuable lessons are yet to come. I have taken Pastor Steve's challenge from Habakkuk 2:2 to heart. I have done my best to inscribe the vision that those who read it will be equipped and empowered to run with us.

When I think about running with the vision, five things come to mind.

1. It's not my vision alone. Yes, I have the passion to see people from every tribe, tongue, and nation born again into the kingdom of God—and to see churches planted that make disciples who make other disciples who plant churches that plant other churches. I do appreciate the leadership team of Every Nation that commissioned me to write this book. However, I feel like one who has been able to see farther and think deeper about missions by simply standing on the shoulders of giants. Though I am, in a sense, a vocal advocate for this Great Commission, the real visionary heroes are campus and church leaders who are called to go into all the world to preach the gospel, make disciples, and plant churches—as well as the local pastors who are willing to send them. We're not just better together; we accomplish little or nothing if we don't embrace and pursue the vision together.

2. My purpose has been to make the vision transportable. When I think of running with a vision, I get a mental picture of a man or woman trying to run a long-distance race with arms full of building blocks. As the runner jumps hurdles, runs through great obstacles, gets lost, or continues through the dark of night, many blocks are dropped along the way. Consequently, some (or even most) of what the runner started out with is lost. Making the vision portable or "graspable" is like putting all the building blocks into one bag so that you can run your race without dropping, losing, or abandoning any of the visionary essentials. That's what I've attempted to do in this book—identify the essential elements of the Every Nation mission and break each one down in order to clarify what they mean and don't mean. My objective has been to make the vision transportable so that those who read it may "run with endurance the race set before them" (Hebrews 12:1).

3. Habakkuk's vision was in the context of judgment. The prophet's chief complaint was that God seemed to sit idly by while the Chaldeans destroyed Jerusalem and carried the children of Israel away into slavery. His primary question was, "God, how could You allow this to happen?" The vision Habakkuk inscribed was one of temporary judgment but eventual victory.

Because I'm an evangelist and not a prophet, I can't tell you what the world or the prospects for global missions will be like in the next twenty-five years. One perspective is that the nations will be ripe for judgment—by political and economic upheaval, because of wars and rumors of wars, and by all manner of spiritual and natural calamities. As a consequence, Christians and missionaries in those nations will feel the effect of God's judgment on that particular nation. Or there could be an era in which the nations are at ease, an era when people are saying "finally, peace and safety"—like the period just before the Lord comes as a "thief in the night" (1 Thessalonians 5:2–4). The next twenty-five years could be the season of the Great Ingathering—of fields that are white and ready for harvest. Or it could be a season of the great "falling away" (2 Thessalonians 2:3, KJV).

Whatever the circumstances of global missions in the coming years, the Great Commission has no expiry date. Our mission remains: to preach the gospel and make disciples of all nations.

4. The challenge of planting churches in every nation will increase significantly. As of this writing, Every Nation has planted churches and campus ministries in eighty of the 195 nations of the world. Many of those nations are open to Christian missionaries. Others are considered creative-access nations, where church planting and evangelism are discouraged, culturally forbidden, or punishable by expulsion or imprisonment. While there are many unrestricted nations and cities that desperately need church-based campus ministries, most of the new churches we will plant in the next twenty-five years will be in creative-access nations, where the levels of risk, faith, prayer, and commitment are greatly increased.

5. We are empowered by clarity of vision. There's an empowering that comes from being filled with the Holy Spirit. There is also an empowerment that comes from having a clear vision of what God has called us to do. How many have prayed, "Lord, I want to do Your will; if I only knew what it was"? Clarity of vision is empowering; lack of clarity is paralyzing.

And so, in a final attempt to run with the vision with you, I hope this book has brought clarity to our mission. I also leave with you the last few pages of this book, which contain a discussion guide that can serve as a practical leadership development exercise.

My challenge for Every Nation leaders is to organize discussion groups for upcoming missionaries, pastors, and leaders. Let them work their way through the discussion questions associated with applications for each chapter. Be sensitive to the Holy Spirit as you pray for the nations, and you can use the Joshua Project as a guide (see Appendix). Following the words of the Apostle Paul, let us entrust what we have heard to faithful men, who will be able to teach others also (2 Timothy 2:2).

DISCUSSION GUIDE

Week 1

READINGS

↗ Introduction to Part One

↗ Chapter 1—Lord of the Harvest

SUMMARY

Jesus challenged His disciples, "Look, I tell you, lift up your eyes, and see that the fields are white for harvest." Jesus seemed to be challenging them to stop filtering the situation of the harvest through the limitations of their own prejudices, inabilities, and expectations, and to embrace a new missionary paradigm—one in which the harvest was seen as white, abundant, and ready for reaping.

LEADERSHIP DISCUSSION

1. In light of the harvest, what do you sense God is calling you to be and do? Do you sense His timing for this?

2. What past experiences have most strengthened or hindered your ability to respond to the readiness of the harvest? Consider the possible effects of having a missions strategy without expectant faith.

3. Discuss some of the pitfalls of missionaries who have struggled with unfruitfulness and jealousy of others' success. What spiritual disciplines will equip you to guard your heart against these pitfalls?

GLOBAL MISSIONS CHALLENGE

Expectations: The primary challenge to Every Nation missionaries is to raise their expectations. Pastor Steve used to remind us regularly, "Don't be satisfied with small successes." William Carey's challenge was "Expect great things from God. Attempt great things for God."

Prayer: Jesus said, "Pray earnestly to the Lord of the harvest to send out laborers into his harvest" (Matthew 9:37,38). We need to be as earnest about our prayers for the Holy Spirit to send laborers as we are about our prayers for the harvest that is already plentiful.

NOTES

Week 2

READING

↗ Chapter 2—Go and Make Disciples

SUMMARY

The Great Commission is not simply going into all the world, and it's not just preaching the gospel or converting nonbelievers to Christ. The great challenge of the Great Commission is making disciples who are equipped and empowered to make other disciples. Effective disciple-making must include these four components: **engaging** culture and community with the gospel, **establishing** biblical foundations, **equipping** believers to minister, and **empowering** disciples to make disciples.

LEADERSHIP DISCUSSION

1. The one essential ingredient for discipleship is a genuine, heartfelt compassion for the lost. Does the ongoing burden for lost souls come easily to you or is it a challenge for you to have this compassion?

2. Discuss your understanding of the four components of discipleship. How can this be contextualized in your city and most effectively employed in your church? Currently, which of the four are the most or least developed in your local church?

3. Discipleship happens in the context of relationships, not programs. Church members develop deep and long-lasting relationships not by simply attending church together, meeting in small groups, or participating together in the work of the ministry, but by sharing life together. How can equipping and empowering members to become actively involved in the work of the ministry strengthen our sense of community? How do we guard discipleship from simply being a program in church that's not based on relationships?

GLOBAL MISSIONS CHALLENGE

Among the greatest and most important challenges for all missionaries, cross-cultural or local, is making disciples in a way that is easily transferable, culturally relevant, and relationship-oriented, which will remain effective no matter the size or diversity of the church.

NOTES

Week 3

READING

↗ Chapter 3—Planting Church-Planting Churches

SUMMARY

Missions for Every Nation can be thought of as three ongoing initiatives: making disciples who are equipped to make other disciples, training leaders who can train other leaders, and planting churches that will plant other churches throughout their respective cities, nations, and regions. The chapter on planting church-planting churches highlights how and why that happens.

LEADERSHIP DISCUSSION

1. Church-planting initiatives create space for the next generation of leaders. Discuss how sending out your top leaders creates opportunities to empower young leaders, compared to being top-heavy in leadership.

2. Church planters work hard at empowering their leadership teams. Discuss the concept of leading with the idea of leaving. If we fail to do so, what would that reveal about our particular church-planting mission?

GLOBAL MISSIONS CHALLENGE

Missionary church planters should begin with a clearly defined vision of what evangelism, discipleship, and church planting would look like in the ideal expression of their church. Visionary leadership is not just promoting ideas; it's instilling, managing, and maintaining ideals.

NOTES

Week 4

READING

↗ Chapter 4—The Great Co-Mission

SUMMARY

We should understand the mission of God in terms of the great "co-mission"—a dual mission of gospel proclamation and gospel demonstration, of preaching the gospel and meeting physical needs among the hearers. Several examples from Every Nation churches are briefly cited along with a discussion of how some movements have diminished or completely abandoned the primary mission of God—the "ministry of reconciliation" (2 Corinthians 5:17–21).

LEADERSHIP DISCUSSION

1. There is no director of social responsibility at Every Nation. Each local church determines the pressing needs of its community and develops the most efficient and effective ways of addressing those needs. Discuss your community's needs and how your church or campus ministry could meet those needs. How will you get involved?

2. Discuss the various aspects of the *missio Dei* (mission of God) in terms of both gospel proclamation and gospel demonstration. How do timing and sequence come into play for your church or campus ministry?

3. Why is establishing a solid biblical foundation essential for all believers, especially for those called to lead social responsibility initiatives?

GLOBAL MISSIONS CHALLENGE

Every Nation pastors, missionaries, and church planters have to discover where, when, and how to invest themselves and their limited resources in compassion ministries. They need to be very clear about their primary calling—they reconcile individuals to God through the gospel and by faith in the finished work of Jesus Christ.

NOTES

Week 5

READINGS

↗ Introduction to Part Two

↗ Chapter 5—Early Church Missionary-Sending Movement

SUMMARY

The chapter begins with a listing of the missionary journeys of the twelve apostles and those known as "the seventy." Most of us have a romanticized understanding of the first-century church and consider it the high-water mark of Christianity. This would mean that Christianity has been on a downward trajectory with regard to power, purity, and influence. Yet nothing could be further from the truth. Christianity spread rapidly, even gaining momentum throughout the second and third centuries. The applications for Every Nation churches and missionaries focus on how and why that happened.

LEADERSHIP DISCUSSION

1. Discuss the dynamics of the gospel dialogues used by the Every Nation church in Madrid. Are you more or less comfortable with open-format dialogues about God, faith, and the gospel?

2. There are many examples of Every Nation missionaries who left well-established churches to start all over again with a new church plant. What is even more remarkable is the number of those who have repeated the process multiple times. Discuss the differences between pioneers and settlers, as well as the personal challenges to going into all the world—again.

3. Sometimes missionaries are led by the Holy Spirit to stand firm amid persecution; other times they are led to flee. With the examples from this chapter in mind, how would you begin to pray through the option of fleeing or persevering?

4. Our philosophy of leadership development is to give disciples the doctrinal foundation and training required to simply take their next step of faith as followers of Christ rather than spending many years in training before engaging in ministry. What are some of the

practical ways Every Nation leaders can employ a grow-as-you-go approach to discipleship?

GLOBAL MISSIONS CHALLENGE

As noted in the foreword by Pastor Steve, we don't exist for the glorious manifestation, but "We exist to honor God by establishing . . . churches and campus ministries . . ." Our global missions approach is what we commonly refer to as the "same old boring strokes." The results are not boring, but the process of making disciples, training leaders, and planting churches is more systematic than mystical. With that being said, we're not following a formula; we're following the Holy Spirit. The more the Holy Spirit demonstrates His presence and power in our midst, the less our approach to global missions will be programmatic and conventional. The global missions challenge for all Every Nation leaders is to be men and women of prayer who are always sensitive to the leading of the Holy Spirit.

NOTES

Week 6

READING

↗ Chapter 6—Moravian Missionary-Sending Movement

SUMMARY

The Moravian Community at Herrnhut in what is today modern Germany was one of church history's most dedicated and courageous missionary-sending movements since the days of the early church. Though the Herrnhut community never grew beyond 600, within a thirty-two-year period they sent out no fewer than 226 missionaries to all parts of the world. By the time of William Carey and the advent of the Modern Missions Movement 150 years later, 2,158 Moravians had already answered the call to serve overseas.

LEADERSHIP DISCUSSION

1. A clear sense of calling enables us to persevere in the face of overwhelming obstacles. At the same time, uncertainty of our calling is among the primary targets of our adversary. How will you respond when faced with these?

2. Many times, people discover their calling only as they take a step of faith to go. Discuss how going and seeing the harvest influences your calling.

3. Nehemiah, Zinzendorf, Leonard Dober, and Demy Reyes all experienced a "holy discontentment" from what they heard or personally experienced. How has an overwhelming burden compelled you to respond?

4. Faith for financial support is a true test of your calling or commitment to it. With regard to finances for yourself or others, what has been your greatest faith challenge? Your greatest victory?

GLOBAL MISSIONS CHALLENGE

"[Jesus] said to all, 'If anyone would come after me, let him deny himself and take up his cross **daily** and follow me'" (Luke 9:23). The global missions challenge is not only to pray with open mind and surrendered heart, "Here I am! Send me" (Isaiah 6:8), but to pray that continually. Denying your own will in order to surrender to God's is a daily battle and a lifelong journey of discipleship.

NOTES

Week 7

READING

↗ Chapter 7—Student Missionary-Sending Movements

SUMMARY

Establishing and sustaining church-based campus ministries has a unique set of challenges. For one, winning and making disciples among nonbelievers on college campuses requires an uncommon measure of boldness, persistence, and faith. Also, since the college-student populations turn over every three or four years, campus missionaries have to continually reach new students and train new leaders. Lastly, a growing church requires effective Every Nation Campus staff who are primarily focused on winning and discipling students.

LEADERSHIP DISCUSSION

Discuss the sacrifices, tensions, and benefits associated with establishing sustainable church-based campus ministries in every nation.

1. **We embrace the tension of being both local and global.** As a worldwide church-planting movement, our mission demands that Every Nation leaders sacrifice by repeatedly sending out and financially supporting their best leaders.

2. **We embrace the tension of being a local church and a church-based campus ministry.** It's a challenge and a sacrifice to focus on a demographic that is such a poor source of funding. In other words, it requires a significant step of faith to plant a church with a primary mission of reaching college students.

3. **We embrace the tension of going and gathering.** Getting together for Every Nation leadership conferences and other staff gatherings costs time and money. However, these are the sacrifices that maintain a movement.

GLOBAL MISSIONS CHALLENGE

The mission of Every Nation: "We exist to honor God by establishing Christ-centered, Spirit-empowered, socially responsible churches and campus ministries in every nation." There are a lot of missionary and church-planting movements located in nations all over the world. I can't say that I'm aware of every single one, but I'm familiar with a great many of them. To my knowledge, Every Nation is one of the few movements dedicated to the mission of systematically planting church-based campus ministries (or campus-ministry-based churches) in every nation. To continue succeeding in that mission requires sacrifice and a great deal of mission focus. However, the benefits are well worth it!

The motto of Every Nation: "Every Nation. Every Campus."

NOTES

Week 8

READING

↗ Chapter 8—Global South Missionary-Sending Movement

SUMMARY

Those paying attention to demographic trends are witnessing a major shift in the global distribution of Christians. While Christianity in the North (Europe and the United States) has been experiencing a steady decline since the 1960s, most of the explosive growth of Christianity is taking place in the global South (Africa, Asia, and Latin America). By the year 2050, four out of five Christians will be from the global South, and the Christian world would have shifted firmly to the southern hemisphere.

LEADERSHIP DISCUSSION

1. With the number of students around the world expected to double by 2025, we need to continue focusing on reaching next-generation leaders. In light of this, what can or should we be doing to creatively engage more students with the gospel?

2. As missionaries are sent into regions of the global South, they will increasingly encounter evil spirits who tenaciously defend their territory and their possessions. Which religious traditions do you feel least equipped to engage for Christ? How can you become a more effective spiritual warrior?

3. Missionaries venturing out into some of the less-Christianized regions of the global South find that apologetics (reasons to believe) is more dependent on demonstrations of the person, power, and presence of Jesus than deductive arguments about the existence of God. In your context, how will you demonstrate the power of the Holy Spirit to meet the needs of others?

GLOBAL MISSIONS CHALLENGE

Globalization is the result of instant access to information, mobile populations, and migration. Consequently, no matter where you live—in London, Nairobi, Nashville, Tehran, or Tokyo—you have to learn about other cultures and be equipped to effectively preach the gospel to people from other religious traditions. More and more, Every Nation missionaries in all regions of the world will regularly interact with Muslims, Hindus, Buddhists, Jews, and agnostics of all types and at all levels of dedication. You cannot pick and choose the ones that God will send your way to hear the gospel. In the words of the Apostle Peter, ". . . always being prepared to make a defense to anyone who asks you for a reason for the hope that is in you; yet do it with gentleness and respect" (1 Peter 3:15).

NOTES

Week 9

READINGS

↗ Introduction to Part Three

↗ Chapter 9—Pray with Expectation

SUMMARY

At the most critical point in our missionary endeavors, there is no organizational strategy (no matter how well conceived) that will give us the direction, boldness, wisdom, provision, or protection that we will need at that moment. That help in times of desperate need will come only from the Helper. This chapter focuses on one critical moment in the history of Christianity, followed by stories from Every Nation. These stories, from both the first and the twenty-first centuries, serve as illustrations of why we must be committed to prayer.

LEADERSHIP DISCUSSION

1. In the New Testament, Spirit-controlled boldness is the result of being filled afresh with the Holy Spirit. Is your understanding and experience of the Holy Spirit that of a one-time event or a repeated infilling? Describe the result of a subsequent infilling of the Holy Spirit.

2. Some of the leaders in the early church were delivered from persecution and even execution; some were not. Many Every Nation missionaries, especially those in creative access nations, face persecution. In light of Jesus' call to count the cost of being His disciple, to what extent are you willing to make a supreme sacrifice for the sake of Christ and the gospel?

3. Sometimes, prayers that prevail are combined with uncommon persistence. Thinking about Dihan's story, describe your most persistent faith challenge that turned into a victory testimony.

4. Wisdom and words will be given to you in the midst of extraordinary situations. With Mark's example in mind, tell about a time when you were a recipient of a supernatural word of wisdom in a desperate situation. For example, have you ever felt a supernatural impression,

like Phuah Boon Leong, to intercede on behalf of someone only to discover that they were in particular need at that very moment?

GLOBAL MISSIONS CHALLENGE

The reasons to pray are just as applicable for those going to Europe, the Americas, or Oceania as they are for those in Africa, Asia, and the Middle East. The only strategy that can help you in those desperate moments is to bathe every aspect of your endeavor in prayer.

NOTES

Week 10

READING

↗ Chapter 10—Give with Generosity

SUMMARY

This chapter recounts how a congregation made up mostly of students made a commitment to look beyond their needs and become a blessing to all nations. Their practical commitment to the Great Commission transformed them from a field nation to a sowing nation.

LEADERSHIP DISCUSSION

1. What is your congregation's level of commitment to give to the Great Commission? What can you do to strengthen the spirit of generosity in your local church?

2. Many of the future Every Nation church plants will be in the regions of the global South. How will you ensure that your church gives to pioneering work in these unreached and restricted regions?

GLOBAL MISSIONS CHALLENGE

As a church-planting movement, our mission is to honor God by establishing churches and campus ministries in every nation. That will never become a reality unless it burns in the hearts of the initial church planter and all subsequent leaders. The practical challenge is to continually keep that vision at the forefront with every member committed to long-term participation by giving sacrificially and generously to the Great Commission.

NOTES

Week 11

READING

↗ Chapter 11—Go with Tenacity

SUMMARY

There have been seasons in church history where world missions was a clearly understood call of the church. Most of that going took place in the first and most recent few centuries. However, there has never been a century in which individuals were not going into all the world, preaching the gospel, and making disciples. This chapter lists some of the most prominent missionaries who have gone tenaciously in the last twenty centuries.

LEADERSHIP DISCUSSION

1. *A Bible and a Passport* is primarily about going into all the world. But more fundamentally, it's about having a missional mindset, which starts with literally having a Bible and a passport. Do you have these? How are you using them? How frequent is your prayer: "Here I am, Lord; send me"?

2. The Greek word *apóstolos* simply means "one who is sent." Whether you are being sent to a neighbor's house or a neighboring nation, you're going as someone sent by and representing Jesus Christ. All disciples are being called to go somewhere or to someone. Where do you think the Holy Spirit is sending you today, next year, or in the years to come?

3. As ambassadors of Christ, we are called to follow Him. But it does not stop there; we also need to heed His command to go into all the world—even into some of the darkest and most difficult places. Discuss the difference between thinking as one who follows and one who is sent. No matter where you are or where you go, Jesus concludes the Great Commission with these words: "Behold, I am with you always, to the end of the age" (Matthew 28:20).

GLOBAL MISSIONS CHALLENGE

The challenge to all Christian disciples then is this: What is the part that you have been called to play? Will you pray, give, and go?

NOTES

APPENDIX

Joshua Project

The Joshua Project[1] is a compilation of statistics on reached and unreached people groups all over the world, focusing on areas with the least number of Christ followers. It can help you as you obey the call of God to bring the gospel to every nation.

COUNTRY	POPULATION	PRIMARY RELIGION	% CHRISTIAN	% EVANGELICAL CHRISTIAN
Afghanistan	36,278,833	Islam	0.06	0.03
Albania	2,902,100	Islam	26.30	0.61
Algeria	41,948,010	Islam	1.48	1.29
American Samoa	55,211	Christianity	95.42	24.84
Andorra	76,378	Christianity	90.60	1.36
Angola	30,718,245	Christianity	91.45	24.31
Anguilla	14,519	Christianity	90.58	33.51
Antigua and Barbuda	101,843	Christianity	92.93	24.85
Argentina	44,616,922	Christianity	93.08	11.04
Armenia	2,888,119	Christianity	94.51	9.67
Aruba	105,069	Christianity	95.48	9.89
Australia	24,688,428	Christianity	65.57	14.46
Austria	8,708,873	Christianity	82.89	0.60
Azerbaijan	9,904,259	Islam	2.65	0.25
Bahamas	396,976	Christianity	94.46	39.66
Bahrain	1,546,278	Islam	8.29	2.50
Bangladesh	165,615,410	Islam	0.34	--

COUNTRY	POPULATION	PRIMARY RELIGION	% CHRISTIAN	% EVANGELICAL CHRISTIAN
Barbados	282,353	Christianity	92.61	33.60
Belarus	9,414,102	Christianity	69.40	1.67
Belgium	11,428,089	Christianity	64.26	1.42
Belize	360,235	Christianity	86.00	23.39
Benin	11,453,095	Christianity	31.57	7.47
Bermuda	59,898	Christianity	91.66	26.31
Bhutan	813,388	Buddhism	0.28	--
Bolivia	11,166,228	Christianity	92.44	19.34
Bosnia-Herzegovina	3,490,440	Islam	44.40	0.17
Botswana	2,270,855	Christianity	65.51	8.26
Brazil	210,725,107	Christianity	89.55	24.56
British Indian Ocean Territory	2,850	Christianity	75.60	32.10
British Virgin Islands	31,282	Christianity	90.66	28.77
Brunei	424,196	Islam	11.70	5.29
Bulgaria	6,992,600	Christianity	82.39	1.98
Burkina Faso	19,705,785	Islam	20.50	10.24
Burundi	11,162,630	Christianity	92.62	29.84
Cambodia	16,195,247	Buddhism	3.17	1.77
Cameroon	24,592,477	Christianity	52.97	9.20
Canada	36,805,641	Christianity	73.47	8.02
Cape Verde	551,590	Christianity	94.87	8.78
Cayman Islands	61,745	Christianity	81.93	21.23
Central African Republic	4,710,191	Christianity	70.40	31.59
Chad	15,292,561	Islam	26.03	7.57
Chile	18,131,255	Christianity	87.12	23.03
China	1,401,453,510	Non-Religious	9.20	7.53

COUNTRY	POPULATION	PRIMARY RELIGION	% CHRISTIAN	% EVANGELICAL CHRISTIAN
China, Hong Kong	7,385,665	Ethnic Religions	12.50	6.03
China, Macau	610,417	Ethnic Religions	5.23	1.78
Christmas Island	1,934	Buddhism	18.93	3.07
Cocos (Keeling) Islands	574	Islam	18.81	3.43
Colombia	49,285,402	Christianity	94.12	10.65
Comoros	825,094	Islam	0.94	0.28
Congo, Democratic Republic of the	83,773,828	Christianity	92.12	19.22
Congo, Republic of the	5,334,317	Christianity	88.24	14.82
Cook Islands	16,622	Christianity	97.66	13.59
Costa Rica	4,917,880	Christianity	95.64	18.35
Côte d'Ivoire	24,850,065	Islam	30.52	9.44
Croatia	4,097,644	Christianity	92.61	0.38
Cuba	11,487,633	Christianity	56.21	11.34
Curacao	160,036	Christianity	85.97	6.86
Cyprus	1,156,592	Christianity	71.91	1.28
Czechia	10,550,124	Non-Religious	26.97	0.74
Denmark	5,740,937	Christianity	82.89	3.62
Djibouti	959,293	Islam	0.86	0.09
Dominica	67,366	Christianity	91.91	17.86
Dominican Republic	10,836,577	Christianity	93.79	10.84
East Timor	1,302,630	Christianity	91.39	2.49
Ecuador	16,810,330	Christianity	93.70	10.57

COUNTRY	POPULATION	PRIMARY RELIGION	% CHRISTIAN	% EVANGELICAL CHRISTIAN
Egypt	99,259,171	Islam	12.66	4.28
El Salvador	6,365,814	Christianity	94.46	44.90
Equatorial Guinea	1,295,848	Christianity	89.84	4.71
Eritrea	5,127,899	Islam	51.04	2.65
Estonia	1,285,540	Non-Religious	48.87	4.45
Ethiopia	107,374,706	Christianity	59.74	17.03
Falkland Islands	2,752	Christianity	64.12	9.06
Faroe Islands	48,068	Christianity	90.91	32.96
Fiji	900,538	Christianity	64.39	26.30
Finland	5,514,408	Christianity	81.47	10.37
France	65,159,520	Christianity	62.34	1.23
French Guiana	287,742	Christianity	81.09	5.55
French Polynesia	280,171	Christianity	83.73	6.11
Gabon	2,037,245	Christianity	75.18	11.93
Gambia	2,128,185	Islam	3.64	0.88
Georgia	3,846,506	Christianity	80.65	1.39
Germany	82,226,255	Christianity	64.37	2.13
Ghana	29,389,523	Christianity	62.42	25.89
Gibraltar	34,393	Christianity	80.47	2.21
Greece	11,109,544	Christianity	88.33	0.49
Greenland	55,866	Christianity	95.32	7.61
Grenada	104,247	Christianity	92.37	18.82
Guadeloupe	406,758	Christianity	95.21	4.77
Guam	157,244	Christianity	92.75	15.66
Guatemala	17,187,655	Christianity	95.53	24.64
Guinea	13,014,529	Islam	4.17	0.69
Guinea-Bissau	1,854,498	Islam	11.77	2.10

COUNTRY	POPULATION	PRIMARY RELIGION	% CHRISTIAN	% EVANGELICAL CHRISTIAN
Guyana	769,398	Christianity	51.44	15.72
Haiti	11,078,521	Christianity	94.84	17.53
Honduras	9,369,398	Christianity	95.86	27.56
Hungary	9,589,959	Christianity	86.79	3.03
Iceland	327,009	Christianity	90.28	4.44
India	1,347,829,801	Hinduism	2.09	--
Indonesia	265,386,196	Islam	12.71	3.18
Iran	81,940,131	Islam	1.34	0.94
Iraq	38,797,313	Islam	1.35	0.20
Ireland	4,753,525	Christianity	91.42	1.56
Isle of Man	82,374	Christianity	65.06	8.47
Israel	8,393,859	Ethnic Religions	1.47	0.42
Italy	59,234,741	Christianity	81.33	1.457
Jamaica	2,883,932	Christianity	81.36	29.75
Japan	127,054,264	Buddhism	2.23	0.58
Jordan	9,825,163	Islam	2.28	0.27
Kazakhstan	18,297,835	Islam	15.28	0.58
Kenya	50,852,115	Christianity	78.03	47.57
Kiribati (Gilbert)	114,617	Christianity	98.41	8.48
Korea, North	25,487,114	Non-Religious	1.66	1.57
Korea, South	51,086,247	Non-Religious	30.10	16.36
Kosovo	1,843,235	Islam	7.01	0.21
Kuwait	4,128,309	Islam	10.07	1.50
Kyrgyzstan	6,066,146	Islam	6.51	0.81
Laos	6,895,193	Buddhism	3.50	2.37
Latvia	1,912,990	Christianity	59.65	7.68
Lebanon	6,058,042	Islam	31.80	0.63
Lesotho	2,236,364	Christianity	92.80	13.33

COUNTRY	POPULATION	PRIMARY RELIGION	% CHRISTIAN	% EVANGELICAL CHRISTIAN
Liberia	4,803,911	Ethnic Religions	39.93	12.57
Libya	6,408,524	Islam	2.18	0.12
Liechtenstein	37,760	Christianity	78.17	0.56
Lithuania	2,847,103	Christianity	84.69	1.41
Luxembourg	552,656	Christianity	80.29	1.00
Macedonia	2,076,483	Christianity	61.99	0.16
Madagascar	26,175,821	Christianity	49.73	6.10
Malawi	19,089,550	Christianity	75.68	17.00
Malaysia	31,981,052	Islam	8.91	3.69
Maldives	437,804	Islam	0.03	0.01
Mali	19,036,981	Islam	2.77	0.66
Malta	414,198	Christianity	96.56	1.54
Marshall Islands	51,170	Christianity	95.23	53.00
Martinique	372,559	Christianity	94.86	6.90
Mauritania	4,510,057	Islam	0.30	0.13
Mauritius	1,230,009	Hinduism	32.62	9.78
Mayotte	251,626	Islam	1.63	0.09
Mexico	130,074,779	Christianity	94.77	10.32
Micronesia, Federated States	103,533	Christianity	95.58	22.76
Moldova	3,966,724	Christianity	75.60	4.67
Monaco	37,685	Christianity	82.57	1.27
Mongolia	3,103,973	Buddhism	2.33	1.72
Montenegro	600,371	Christianity	74.25	0.26
Montserrat	5,043	Christianity	94.94	27.46
Morocco	36,102,854	Islam	0.19	0.10
Mozambique	30,453,923	Christianity	52.79	13.34

COUNTRY	POPULATION	PRIMARY RELIGION	% CHRISTIAN	% EVANGELICAL CHRISTIAN
Myanmar (Burma)	53,757,100	Buddhism	7.96	4.66
Namibia	2,558,052	Christianity	89.79	13.77
Nauru	10,513	Christianity	85.66	12.60
Nepal	29,496,002	Hinduism	1.19	--
Netherlands	16,981,968	Non-Religious	47.20	4.24
New Caledonia	273,590	Christianity	79.58	6.18
New Zealand	4,696,160	Christianity	52.63	18.56
Nicaragua	6,224,910	Christianity	96.26	42.97
Niger	22,253,526	Islam	1.51	0.92
Nigeria	195,652,488	Christianity	50.64	25.54
Niue	1,543	Christianity	95.89	5.43
Norfolk Island	1,615	Christianity	72.27	20.43
Northern Mariana Islands	52,707	Christianity	74.96	16.82
Norway	5,291,297	Christianity	88.54	8.13
Oman	4,772,276	Islam	2.71	0.80
Pakistan	199,926,353	Islam	0.71	--
Palau	21,326	Christianity	95.51	21.96
Panama	4,157,678	Christianity	88.18	21.58
Papua New Guinea	8,332,453	Christianity	95.86	22.80
Paraguay	6,869,812	Christianity	95.39	8.08
Peru	32,501,838	Christianity	94.56	14.41
Philippines	106,356,453	Christianity	90.97	13.93
Pitcairn Islands	48	Christianity	96.00	10.00
Poland	38,000,934	Christianity	89.58	0.31
Portugal	10,210,981	Christianity	93.35	3.36
Puerto Rico	3,622,360	Christianity	94.56	32.67
Qatar	2,565,487	Islam	6.29	0.85

COUNTRY	POPULATION	PRIMARY RELIGION	% CHRISTIAN	% EVANGELICAL CHRISTIAN
Reunion	872,673	Christianity	85.55	6.80
Romania	19,521,337	Christianity	93.69	6.34
Russia	142,657,014	Christianity	57.66	1.46
Rwanda	12,382,808	Christianity	88.95	26.24
Saint Helena	3,962	Christianity	94.99	8.80
Saint Kitts and Nevis	55,431	Christianity	92.53	22.01
Saint Lucia	175,964	Christianity	94.89	18.28
Saint Pierre and Miquelon	6,130	Christianity	96.49	0.62
Samoa	194,574	Christianity	96.17	18.57
San Marino	33,377	Christianity	84.11	0.07
São Tomé and Príncipe	205,336	Christianity	85.69	5.88
Saudi Arabia	33,461,416	Islam	4.34	0.56
Senegal	16,228,759	Islam	4.48	0.17
Serbia	6,822,007	Christianity	79.21	0.72
Seychelles	92,461	Christianity	96.18	6.96
Sierra Leone	7,682,704	Islam	13.27	4.97
Singapore	5,756,568	Buddhism	13.26	7.37
Sint Maarten	40,343	Christianity	88.61	7.88
Slovakia	5,393,401	Christianity	92.78	1.42
Slovenia	2,057,374	Christianity	54.06	0.21
Solomon Islands	610,182	Christianity	96.10	31.20
Somalia	15,065,395	Islam	0.28	0.01
South Africa	57,295,550	Christianity	77.48	21.13
South Sudan	12,795,068	Christianity	57.68	11.30
Spain	46,320,057	Christianity	77.55	1.60
Sri Lanka	20,831,516	Buddhism	7.60	--

COUNTRY	POPULATION	PRIMARY RELIGION	% CHRISTIAN	% EVANGELICAL CHRISTIAN
St Vincent and Grenadines	106,567	Christianity	88.78	41.03
Sudan	41,393,420	Islam	5.04	0.38
Suriname	534,372	Christianity	46.98	17.62
Svalbard	2,642	Christianity	90.99	6.68
Swaziland	1,329,189	Christianity	84.06	20.80
Sweden	9,931,082	Christianity	55.68	5.79
Switzerland	8,472,866	Christianity	76.55	3.95
Syria	18,197,880	Islam	5.72	0.19
Taiwan	23,648,674	Ethnic Religions	5.96	3.30
Tajikistan	9,062,469	Islam	1.00	0.12
Tanzania	59,032,009	Christianity	51.65	11.11
Thailand	69,037,699	Buddhism	1.26	0.63
Togo	7,942,967	Christianity	45.31	10.99
Tokelau	1,268	Christianity	100.00	3.40
Tonga	105,691	Christianity	95.87	15.69
Trinidad and Tobago	1,362,215	Christianity	66.12	23.44
Tunisia	11,631,663	Islam	0.42	0.03
Turkey	81,863,602	Islam	0.66	0.04
Turkmenistan	5,796,933	Islam	4.44	0.10
Turks and Caicos Islands	35,023	Christianity	90.67	31.96
Tuvalu	10,754	Christianity	98.00	22.83
Uganda	44,234,744	Christianity	83.51	33.85
Ukraine	43,942,853	Christianity	72.97	3.62
United Arab Emirates	10,375,659	Islam	8.17	1.38

COUNTRY	POPULATION	PRIMARY RELIGION	% CHRISTIAN	% EVANGELICAL CHRISTIAN
United Kingdom	66,468,577	Christianity	57.00	7.89
United States	325,627,248	Christianity	77.31	26.40
Uruguay	3,445,088	Christianity	66.76	7.29
Uzbekistan	32,301,826	Islam	4.39	0.24
Vanuatu	280,001	Christianity	91.83	41.28
Vatican City	798	Christianity	100.00	2.50
Venezuela	32,310,531	Christianity	82.56	12.19
Vietnam	96,418,609	Buddhism	10.14	2.39
Virgin Islands (U.S.)	103,476	Christianity	94.22	24.37
Wallis and Futuna Islands	11,715	Christianity	98.48	1.75
West Bank / Gaza	5,011,960	Islam	1.25	0.07
Western Sahara	561,935	Islam	0.03	0.0008
Yemen	28,759,437	Islam	0.22	0.03
Zambia	17,537,015	Christianity	86.98	25.15
Zimbabwe	16,845,357	Christianity	76.65	25.23

REFERENCES

PART ONE: THE CALL TO EVERY NATION

1. George Smith, *The Life of William Carey: Shoemaker & Missionary* (New York: E.P. Dutton, 1909), 31–32.

2. Smith, *The Life of William Carey: Shoemaker & Missionary*.

Chapter 1: Lord of the Harvest

Chapter 2: Go and Make Disciples

1. Peter Steinfels, "Beliefs; Millennial Fears in the Year 1000: Apocalypse then, Apocalypse now and Apocalypse Forever," *New York Times*, July 17, 1999.

2. Steve Murrell, *WikiChurch: Making Discipleship Engaging, Empowering, & Viral* (Lake Mary: Charisma House, 2011), 56.

3. Peter F. Drucker, *Management: Tasks, Responsibilities, Practices*, 1st ed. (New York: Rouledge, 2012), 361.

Chapter 3: Planting Church-Planting Churches

1. Ferdie Cabiling, *RUN: Endure the Pain, Keep the Faith, Finish Your Race* (Manila: Every Nation Productions, 2018), 103–104.

Chapter 4: The Great Co-Mission

1. Tormod Engelsviken, "Missio Dei: The Understanding and Misunderstanding of a Theological Concept in European Churches and Missiology," *International Review of Mission* 92, no. 367 (October 2003): 482.

2. John F. Hoffmeyer, "The Missional Trinity," *Dialog: A Journal of Theology* 40, no. 2 (June 2001): 108.

PART TWO: MISSIONARY-SENDING MOVEMENTS

Chapter 5: Early Church Missionary-Sending Movement

1. Rodney Stark, *The Rise of Christianity: How the Obscure, Marginal Jesus Movement Became the Dominant Religious Force in the Western World in a Few Centuries* (Princeton: Princeton University Press, 1996).

2. "Evangelism in the Early Church: Did You Know?" *Christian History* no. 57 (1998).

3. E. Glenn Hinson, "Ordinary Saints at First Church," *Christian History* no. 57 (1998).

4. Robert L. Wilken, "Evangelism in the Early Church: Christian History Interview - Roman Redux," *Christian History* no. 57 (1998).

5. D.A. Carson, *The Expositor's Bible Commentary*, ed. Frank E. Gaebelein, (1982) s.v. "Matthew."

6. *The Apostolic Tradition of Hippolytus*, trans. Burton Scott Easton (New York: Cambridge University Press, 1934).

Chapter 6: Moravian Missionary-Sending Movement

1. Leslie K. Tarr, "A Prayer Meeting that Lasted 100 Years," *Christian History* 1, no. 1 (1982).

2. C.G.A. Oldendorp, "Missionaries against Terrible Odds," *History of the Mission of the Evangelical Brethren to the Caribbean Islands of St. Thomas, St. Croix, and St. John*, ed. Johann Jakob Bossart, trans. Arnold R. Highfield and Vladimir Barac (Ann Arbor: Karoma Publishers, 1987).

3. Todd M. Johnson and Gina A. Zurlo, eds. *World Christian Database* (Leiden/Boston: Brill, 2018).

4. Oldendorp, "Missionaries against Terrible Odds," *History of the Mission of the Evangelical Brethren to the Caribbean Islands of St. Thomas, St. Croix, and St. John*.

5. Ferdie Cabiling, *RUN: Endure the Pain, Keep the Faith, Finish Your Race* (Manila: Every Nation Productions, 2018), 97.

6. "The Rich Young Ruler . . . Who Said Yes!" *Christian History* 1, no. 1 (1982).

Chapter 7: Student Missionary-Sending Movements

1. John Pollock, *The Cambridge Seven: The True Story of Ordinary Men Used in No Ordinary Way* (Feam: Christian Focus Publications, 2006).

2. Michael Parker, "Mobilizing a Generation for Missions," *Christian History*, August 6, 2009, https://www.christianitytoday.com/history/2009/august/mobilizing-generation-for-missions.html.

3. "Decision on Mount Hermon," *The Yale Standard*, February 28, 2012, http://www.yalestandard.com/histories/decision-on-mount-hermon/.

4. Trent Sheppard, *God on Campus: Sacred Causes & Global Effects* (Downers Grove: InterVarsity Press, 2009), 100.

5. Parker, "Mobilizing a Generation for Missions."

6. *Perspective on the World Christian Movement: A Reader*, ed. Ralph D. Winter and Steven C. Hawthorne (Pasadena: William Carey Library, 1981).

7. Steve Murrell, *100 Years from Now: Sustaining a Movement for Generations* (Nashville: Dunham Books, 2013), 147–148.

8. "Ministry Impact," About Us, InterVarsity, accessed January 10, 2019, https://intervarsity.org/about-us/ministry-impact.

9. Peter J. Wells, "The Role of Quality Assurance in Higher Education: Challenges, Developments and Trends" (PowerPoint presentation, UNESCO Regional Meeting on QA, Moscow Russia Federation, April 2018).

10. "Why the Campus," Campus Ministry, Every Nation, accessed January 10, 2019, https://www.everynation.org/about/campus-ministry/.

Chapter 8: Global South Missionary-Sending Movement

1. Dave Hazzan, "Christianity and Korea," *The Diplomat*, April 7, 2016, https://thediplomat.com/2016/04/christianity-and-korea/.

2. Jae Kyeong Lee, "Why Does South Korea Send Out So Many Missionaries?" *God Reports*, February 28, 2018, https://blog.godreports.com/2018/02/why-does-south-korea-send-out-so-many-missionaries/.

3. Melissa Steffan, "The Surprising Countries Most Missionaries Are Sent From and Go To," News & Reporting, *Christianity Today*, July 25, 2013, https://www.christianitytoday.com/news/2013/july/missionaries-countries-sent-received-csgc-gordon-conwell.html.

4. Todd M. Johnson and Gina A. Zurlo, eds. *World Christian Database* (Leiden/Boston: Brill, 2018).

5. Johnson and Zurlo, eds. *World Christian Database*.

6. John Mbiti as quoted by Kwame Bediako, *Christianity in Africa: The Renewal of a Non-Western Religion* (Edinburgh: Orbis Books, 1995), 154.

7. Jim Ramsay, "Paradigm Shifts in Global Missions Every Christian Should Know," *Seedbed*, April 11, 2016, https://www.seedbed.com/paradigm-shifts-in-global-missions-2/.

8. Johnson and Zurlo, eds. *World Christian Database*.

9. Philip Jenkins, *The Next Christendom: The Coming of Global Christianity* (Oxford: Oxford University Press, 2002), 253.

10. Johnson and Zurlo, eds. *World Christian Database*.

11. Jenkins, *The Next Christendom: The Coming of Global Christianity*, 16.

12. "America's Changing Religious Landscape," *Religion & Public Life*, *Pew Research Center*, May 12, 2015, http://www.pewforum.org/2015/05/12/americas-changing-religious-landscape/.

13. Ed Stetzer, "Nominals to Nones: 3 Key Takeaways from Pew's Religious Landscape Survey," *Christianity Today*, May 12, 2015, https://www.christianitytoday.com/edstetzer/2015/may/nominals-to-nones-3-key-takeaways-from-pews-religious-lands.html.

14. Samuel Stebbins, "The Most Religious Counties of Every State in the U.S." *USA Today*, March 13, 2018, https://www.usatoday.com/story/news/2018/03/13/most-religious-counties-every-state-u-s/421946002/.

PART THREE: FULFILLING THE EVERY NATION MISSION

Chapter 9: Pray with Expectation

1. Steve Murrell, *100 Years from Now: Sustaining a Movement for Generations* (Nashville: Dunham Books, 2013), 41.

2. Compass Direct News, "Top 10 Persecution Stories of 2008," *Christian Headlines*, January 12, 2009. https://www.christianheadlines.com/news/top-10-persecution-stories-of-2008-11597966.html.

Chapter 10: Give with Generosity

1. Ferdie Cabiling, *RUN: Endure the Pain, Keep the Faith, Finish Your Race* (Manila: Every Nation Productions, 2018), 109.

Chapter 11: Go with Tenacity

1. Tony Mariot, "Where Did Each of the Apostles Travel after Christ's Ascension?" *Quora*, updated November 22, 2017, https://www.quora.com/Where-did-each-of-the-apostles-travel-after-Christs-ascension.

2. *Ante-Nicene Fathers vol. 5*, ed. Alexander Roberts, Sir James Donaldson, and A. Cleveland Coxe (New York: Christian Literature Publishing Co., 1999), 245–246.

3. *Nicene and Post-Nicene Fathers: Second Series, Volume VI Jerome: Letters and Select Works*, ed. Philip Schaff (New York: Cosimo Inc., 2007).

4. Rodney Stark, *The Rise of Christianity: How the Obscure, Marginal Jesus Movement Became the Dominant Religious Force in the Western World in a Few Centuries* (Princeton: Princeton University Press, 1996).

5. Rev. Alban Butler, "St. Dionysius, Bishop of Paris, and His Companions, Martyrs," *The Lives of the Saints* (Dublin: James Duffy, 1866).

6. *Encyclopaedia Britannica*, online ed. (2019), s.v. "Saint-Pachomius."

7. "The Spread of Christianity through Persecutions," *Holy Monastery of Pantokrator*, accessed January 10, 2019, https://www.impantokratoros.gr/spread-christianity-persecutions. en.aspx.

8. "Saint Patrick," *Catholic Online*, accessed January 10, 2019, https://www.catholic.org/saints/saint.php?saint_id=89.

9. Todd Johnson and Sun Young Chung, "Tracking Global Christianity's Statistical Centre of Gravity, AD 33–AD 2100," *International Review of Mission* 93, no. 369 (March 2009).

10. "The Spread of Christianity through Persecutions," *Holy Monastery of Pantokrator*.

11. Christian History Magazine Editorial Staff, *131 Christians Everyone Should Know*, ed. Mark Galli and Ted Olsen (Nashville: Broadman & Holman Publishers, 2000).

12. "SS. Cyril and Methodius: The Apostles and Teachers of the Ruthenian People," *Archeparchy of Pittsburgh*, accessed January 10, 2019, http://www.archpitt.org/ss-cyril-and-methodius-the-apostles-and-teachers-of-the-ruthenian-people/.

13. Christian History Magazine Editorial Staff, *131 Christians Everyone Should Know.*

14. Roald Berg, "The Missionary Impulse in Norwegian History," *Studia Historiae Ecclesiasticae* 36, no. 1 (May 2010).

15. "700-year-old Gospel Challenge in Mongolia is Answered," *Christian Examiner*, January 17, 2009, https://www.gordonconwell.edu/ockenga/research/documents/StatusofGlobalChristianity2018.pdf.

16. Dan Graves, "Raymond Lull, Troubadour for God," *Christianity.com*, updated June 2007, https://www.christianity.com/church/church-history/timeline/1201-1500/raymond-lull-troubadour-for-god-11629855.html.

17. "Printing Press," *The Great Idea Finder*, revised May 1, 2007, http://www.ideafinder.com/history/inventions/printpress.htm.

18. "Global Christianity," *Religion & Public Life, Pew Research Center*, December 1, 2014, http://www.pewforum.org/interactives/global-christianity/#/Democratic%20Republic%20of%20the%20Congo,Catholic.

19. Johnson and Chung, "Tracking Global Christianity's Statistical Centre of Gravity, AD 33–AD 2100."

20. Johnson and Chung, "Tracking Global Christianity's Statistical Centre of Gravity, AD 33–AD 2100."

21. Joshua Claycamp, "Thanks Giving: Holding the Rope," *First Baptist Bloggage*, First Baptist Church, October 8, 2012, http://www.firstbaptistkamloops.org/first-baptist-bloggage/thanks-giving-holding-the-rope/.

22. Andrea Servant, "Devotional—Holding the Ropes," *YWAM Gateway*, accessed January 10, 2019, https://ywamgateway.hk/news/devotional-holding-the-ropes/.

AFTERWORD: Equip the Next Generation

1. Stephen R. Covey, *The 7 Habits of Highly Effective People: Restoring the Character Ethic*, 1st ed. (New York: Simon & Schuster, 1989).

APPENDIX: Joshua Project

1. "All People Groups by Country," Resources, Datasets, Joshua Project, accessed December 10, 2018, https://joshuaproject.net/resources/datasets.